Dedication

This book is dedicated to my father, Jim Rorie. Dad, you did a great job of passing the torch to me. I love you. It is also dedicated to Daniel Rorie, my beloved son in whom I am well pleased. You came like a gift to us and every day I become prouder to be called your Dad. I love you.

I would like to gratefully acknowledge the men in my life who have fathered me, mentored me, been my friend and shown me, maybe even unwittingly, what real men do. You will hear their voices in every chapter.

These are men like R.O. Rorie, Jim Rorie, Joe Rorie, Larry Rorie, R.A. Prather, Dr. Edwin Louis Cole, Dr. Paul Louis Cole, Pastor G.F. Watkins, Ps. Eugene Green, Sean Moss, Jack King, Mark Robison, Mitch Mullin, Greg Brinkley, Doug Thompson, Rick Johnson, Pastor Tim Cross, Pastor Randy Huett, Pastor Josh Moran, and Constantine Antos.

I have been honored to be in relationship with these men at different crucial stages of my life and am thankful for their wisdom and influence.

I am also thankful to Clinton Etheridge and Marnie Scarborough for help in editing and to Keith and Marnie Scarborough for your help in making this book possible.

PASSING THE TORCH OF MANHOOD

A Father & Son Adventure

13-Week Study in Biblical Manhood

By Tony Rorie

© 2014 Tony Rorie

Honor Books

ISBN 10: 1-60796-761-8
ISBN 13: 978-1-60796-761-3

Published by Honor Books – Masterpiece Printing & Graphics, Inc., Dallas, TX 75207

www.tonyrorie.com
www.thetorchofmanood.com

Printed in the United States of America

Endorsements

Tony Rorie is radically changing the lives of more boys (and men) than anyone else I know. In *Passing the Torch* he has developed a masterpiece to give men the tools they need to help guide their sons or any boy who needs their guidance into the dangerous world of authentic manhood. I am excited to see the impact this devotional is going to have in the lives of men and boys around the world.

– Rick Johnson

Bestselling author of *Better Dads Stronger Sons,*
A Man in the Making, and *The Power of a Man*

In a day when young men and boys are desperate for fathers and fathers are desperate for help, my friend and brother Tony Rorie has created a tool every father should have and every son needs to hear. *"Passing the Torch"* is like having an M60 machine gun in a knife fight. Tony has years of experience transforming the lives of young men and boys.

This study should be mandatory for every man in church and every man should be required to lead another young man in this study. Do not miss this opportunity to help change the life and direction of a young man.

– Dr. Chuck Stecker
President & Founder, A Chosen Generation &
The Center for InterGenerational Ministry

"One of the most exhilarating things a man can do is come alongside a younger man and help him step into manhood. This is obviously a mandate for fathers but with tools like "Passing the Torch" any man can come alongside and step into a young man's life. Tools like this study help men move from good intention into good execution. You don't need to figure out what to do. Grab a couple young men and a couple copies of *Passing the Torch*" and make your impact on eternity!"

– Brian Doyle
Founder and President, Iron Sharpens Iron

Tony Rorie knows how to develop men. In this very practical and insightful book, dads will find an easy to follow blueprint for intentional investment in the lives of their sons. This type of investment doesn't leave the development of their character to chance and ensure a strong legacy for the generations that follow. Intentional parenting in the way that Tony outlines and facilitates through this book is a Kingdom basic and absolutely necessary in this age where our children are under constant assault. This book will make sons and fathers better individually and stronger relationally.

– Ps. Scott Prickett

Men's Pastor – Bold Men Northwood Church, Keller TX

Tony Rorie understands mentoring. Tony's life is a great living example of what he writes in "Passing the Torch." He had a great father as a role model. Now Tony has used this model to pass the torch to his son and daughters. Furthermore, Tony has went beyond his immediate family and mentored many more young men that God has placed in his path. Tony shares his love and passion for our true mentor in every situation which is Jesus. It is this love and passion that has driven Tony to share this with us in this writing.

– Darrel Billups, Th.D.

NCMM, Executive Director

National Coalition of Ministries to Men

Tony Rorie has been a friend of mine for many years. We met around an Ed Cole gathering which dealt with men taking responsibility. That should tell you a little about what he has been chasing.

I believe in Tony's calling with men of all ages but am extremely excited about this book and its potential when it comes to helping men with their sons. We hear a lot of speeches and sermons on what we ought to be doing as men to help our sons, in a general way. However, "Passing the Torch," gives us practical tools when mentoring our sons.

Thank you Tony for caring for me and for men around the world!

– G.F. Watkins
Pastor, Author, Founder of Jordan Ranch

TABLE OF CONTENTS

Foreword by Jeff Kemp

Foreword by Jeff Kemp

Do you have a voice that echoes in your spirit? Did you hear the golden words "You have what it takes, Son, I'm proud of the man you are. I love you." My dad was an NFL quarterback and a visible public figure, but as he was dying from cancer he stressed to me that his greatest joy and only legacy that mattered was his family.

My dad had his blind spots and flaws, as we all do, but he was a champion encourager. My dad was at all my games, he prioritized the dinner table and family conversation, and he exposed us kids to world leaders and adult ideas. He hugged and kissed us and the words "I love you" flowed freely in our home. I received frequent notes and phone calls reminding me that, "God has a plan. You are in your right place. You're a Kemp, be a leader. You're day will come. Never quit. Let your light shine so that your heavenly father is glorified." My life and leadership has been shaped by my epic-encouraging dad.

You dads reading this need to know that you mean the world to your sons! This book will help you give your son that voice that keeps echoing through the years.

Nothing I've done in life is as important as my fatherhood mission of shaping four sons to be men who know God, love God and live their calling. For us, the highlights have been family dinners, taking sons to breakfast and our special welcome to manhood trips at age 13 and 18. My big prayer is that my sons will know me and that I will know them, and most importantly that they will know and live through Jesus and His word. I want to encourage you that prayer is your # 1 role as a dad...prayer for God's work in their hearts and character...and prayer for wisdom in your fathering and man training.

There are some things I did not do as well as I'd like to have done, and this book is a big part of the answer. Tony Rorie is a role model of fathering and mentoring. He's honest and encourages us dads to be the same. Passing the torch gives a dad a straightforward, clear playbook for pointing your son to godly manhood. It's awesome because it is powered by scripture, but anchored in relationship.

This refreshingly short book is perfect for opening up the most important conversations a dad and son want to have. It will help you take your son through great scripture and core character traits of manhood. Use it as a chance to reveal yourself to your son...your past fears and failings, your errors and lessons, and your love...for your God and for them. Don't be afraid to apologize. And get ready to call them up into manhood.

We're all flawed in our own way. Don't beat yourself up over the past. Turn to the Lord and seize every day God gives you from here on out. Point your sons to Jesus and becoming a man whose identity and character are in Christ.

You don't need to be the fastest, but you do need to hand off the baton of faith. You don't need to be the best QB, but you do need to complete the pass to your son. You don't need to be the brightest light, but you do need to pass the torch. Jesus is the fire, the role model of a man and the source of the character you want to pass on to your son.

Dads, I'm excited for you and proud of you. God will guide you as you open the conversation, follow this biblical man plan, and do your greatest mission...build your son into a man.

Jeff Kemp, former NFL Quarterback, Vice President at Family Life and author of *Facing The Blitz.*

We are so excited that you are starting this journey together as Father & Son. In each chapter, you will find four key points about that particular aspect of manhood and also four key Bible verses.

The ideal age for your son to go through this material with you is 9-16. However, you can feel confident that it will be an amazing experience for you and your son all the way up until his 21st birthday. In the last chapter, there is a rite of passage that you can do together to authenticate and forever solidify your son's entrance into manhood.

Hopefully, you can find a place for the two of you to be alone each week or together with a group to focus on the chapter. Begin each chapter by reading the material together and stop to discuss any questions that might come up as you read. At the end of the chapter, there will be activities for Dad, son, and also activities to be completed together as a team.

One practical aspect we'd like to mention is that each chapter doesn't necessarily have to be completed in a week, as some of the projects will take some time. Simply move at your own pace or the pace of your group.

Note: We want to challenge you to be as transparent and honest with your son concerning key areas of manhood and your experience. The amount of truth you are willing to share is proportionate to the freedom that will come from the study.

"And you will know the truth, and the truth will set you free." (John 8:32)

LESSON 1

THE DEFINITION OF MANHOOD

A Young Theodore Roosevelt - Britannica

If

BY RUDYARD KIPLING

If you can keep your head when all about you

    Are losing theirs and blaming it on you,

If you can trust yourself when all men doubt you,

    But make allowance for their doubting too;

If you can wait and not be tired by waiting,

    Or being lied about, don't deal in lies,

Or being hated, don't give way to hating,

    And yet don't look too good, nor talk too wise:

If you can dream—and not make dreams your master;

    If you can think—and not make thoughts your aim;

If you can meet with Triumph and Disaster

    And treat those two impostors just the same;

If you can bear to hear the truth you've spoken

    Twisted by knaves to make a trap for fools,

Or watch the things you gave your life to, broken,

    And stoop and build 'em up with worn-out tools:

If you can make one heap of all your winnings

And risk it on one turn of pitch-and-toss,

And lose, and start again at your beginnings

And never breathe a word about your loss;

If you can force your heart and nerve and sinew

To serve your turn long after they are gone,

And so hold on when there is nothing in you

Except the will which says to them: 'Hold on!'

If you can talk with crowds and keep your virtue,

Or walk with Kings—nor lose the common touch,

If neither foes nor loving friends can hurt you,

If all men count with you, but none too much;

If you can fill the unforgiving minute

With sixty seconds' worth of distance run,

Yours is the Earth and everything that's in it,

And—which is more—you'll be a Man, my son!

Source: A Choice of Kipling's Verse (1943)

Manhood

"Manhood and Christ-likeness are synonymous."

– Ed Cole

In this segment we will discuss together the true meaning of Biblical manhood by looking at Jesus, the true model for masculinity and manhood.

Four Key Points on Manhood

I. Jesus Was *and Is* THE Standard of Manhood

II. The True Measure of a Man is His Service to Others

III. We are Male by Birth, Man by Choice

IV. Manhood can Sometime be A Dangerous Thing

Four Key Verses on Manhood

I. *We do this by keeping our eyes on Jesus, the champion who initiates and perfects our faith. Because of the joy awaiting him, he endured the cross, disregarding its shame. Now he is seated in the place of honor beside God's throne. (Hebrews 12:2)*

II. *Then Jesus came out wearing the crown of thorns and the purple robe. And Pilate said, "Look, here is the man!" (John 19:5)*

III. *The members of the Council were amazed when they saw the boldness of Peter and John, for they could see that they were ordinary men with no special training in the Scriptures. They also recognized them as men who had been with Jesus. (Acts 4:13)*

IV. *"Jesus made a whip from some ropes and chased them all out of the Temple. He drove out the sheep and cattle, scattered the moneychangers' coins over the floor, and turned over their tables. (John 2:15)*

Manhood Key Point I:

Jesus Was *and Is* the Pattern of Manhood

Have you ever stopped and wondered as you were putting gas in the car, "Am I really getting the amount of gas that it says on this meter?" Have you ever wondered if you were really getting your monies worth? Unless you've actually pulled out a gallon measure and checked for yourself, you are just taking the gas station's word for it.

Fortunately, there is a certifying body that regularly monitors the weights and measures of scales and meters and certifies with their official seal that the instrument has been calibrated using a "Master Standard". Just look on the pump the next time you get gas.

All things have to be measured by a true or master standard. Manhood is no different. The problem with culture today is that there are a large number of standards for manhood and the majority of them are incorrect.

It wasn't until I asked Jesus to be the Lord and Savior of my life, and began studying God's word that I began to fully learn that Manhood and Christ-likeness are synonymous, or *the same thing*. When we begin to apply the Biblical definitions of manhood, we will prosper and our hearts will come alive. We become Christ-like men.

In the Gospel accounts of Jesus, we find an interesting encounter between Jesus and a Roman ruler in Jerusalem. This encounter gave the ruler a true definition of what it meant to be a man.

Pilate was sitting in his judgment seat on the pavement, outside the Praetorium listening to an endless litany of cases referred to him from all over his province.

He sat motionless as the delegates of the conquered Jewish nation presented each complaint and detail of injustice.

Judea had become a hotbed of insurrection and Pilate had been threatened twice by Herod to maintain the peace at all costs. He could not afford another uprising.

The screaming crowd, led by the ruling members of Israel's ruling body, the Sanhedrin, was growing increasingly angry as they led the latest object of unrest and complaint to Pilate's judgment seat.

What had this man done to deserve the anger and bitter persecution displayed by the mob behind him? Pilate, not wanting to deal with this situation, had already had him sent to Herod for his thoughts on the matter.

Herod had found no fault in him and, for that matter, neither could Pilate.

He had been warned of his wife who had a very troubling dream concerning this same Jesus. She told him, "Have nothing to do with that righteous man!"

But yet, here he was. Pilate had spoken briefly with him in private to see if the allegations were true.

"There was no fear in his eyes as he answered my questions," Pilate thought. There were no attempts of blame shifting or complaints. There was only a passionate reply pointing to truth and principle. This was no ordinary man.

Pilate therefore said to Him, "Are you a king then?"

Jesus answered, "You say *rightly* that I am a king. For this cause I was born and for this cause I have come into the world, that I should bear witness to the truth. Everyone who is of the truth hears My voice." Pilate said to Him, "What is truth?" And when he had said this, he went out again to the Jews, and said to them, "I find no fault in Him at all." (John 18:37-38 NKJV)

Pilate brought him back before the crowd and presented Jesus to the crowd with a Latin phrase. "Ecce Homo!" meaning, "Behold, *THE* man...."

Jesus was the prototype of what a man should be, embodying all the attributes of true manhood. His pattern for manhood was very obvious and evident for all to hear and see. His pattern of life, love for others, and selfless sacrifice embody the greatest and best of manhood. We need look no further to find the true definition of manhood. Jesus is our example.

One of the strongest and most obvious proofs of manhood is a man's desire to help and protect others, which brings us to our second characteristic of manhood.

Manhood Key Point II:

The True Measure of a Man is His Service to Others

A great man is great, because he is mature. He becomes mature because he is willing to take responsibility for others.

I especially like a scene from the movie "10,000 BC". In this scene, the uncle (TicTic) is describing to his nephew D'Leh the character of D'Leh's father, who had gone missing. He was describing the character that he showed by taking responsibility for the other members of their tribe.

"A good man draws a circle around himself and cares for those within; His woman, his children. Other men draw a larger circle and bring within their brothers and sisters.
But some men have a great destiny. They must draw around themselves a circle that includes many, many more. Your father was one of those men. You must decide for yourself whether you are, as well."

Jesus was great. He was great because he was mature. He was mature because he took responsibility not for his own sins, but the sins of the world. He took responsibility not just for himself; He took responsibility for all creation. That's what made him fully man and fully mature.

Jesus grew in maturity wisdom & stature because of the things he suffered. Adversity builds great men. Embracing crisis and adversity as an opportunity to grow helps us grow strong and rise in stature. When we take our eyes off from ourselves and put them on those around us, we become like Jesus and become mature.

Abraham Lincoln once said, "A man is never so tall, as when he stoops to help a child."

We demonstrate the power of being a man by helping others and serving our fellow man.

A child is the center of his own universe, demands his own way, and pouts and throws a tantrum when things don't go his way. But a man, by contrast, demonstrates his maturity by his consideration for others. If you want to be mature, take responsibility. If you want to be great, take responsibility for the welfare of others.

General William Booth was the founder of The Salvation Army, a now global organization that helps the less fortunate and provides aid for the needy. Toward the end of his life, General Booth became very ill and was not able to attend the convention of the growing organization that he led. During these days there was no video or audio technology available to allow him to communicate to his group, only telegraph.

The expense was great to send a communication to his workers all over the globe, so his message to them would have to be condensed down to only one word. What word would he choose to convey the message of their mission? What word would he choose to encourage the workers all over the world? Here was his original message:

Dear Delegates of the Salvation Army Convention:

OTHERS!

Signed, General Booth

A real man thinks of others more than he thinks of himself. He has found the true joy in life; it is better to give than receive!

Manhood Key Point III:

We are Male by Birth, Man by Choice

You can be a male, but not be a man. True manhood requires a choice to live manly and not like a child any longer. The Apostle Paul tells us that "When I was a child, I spoke and thought and reasoned as a child. But when I grew up, I put away childish things." (1 Corinthians 13:11)

I find it interesting that it describes a child as speaking first then thinking, then acting, while the opposite would be true for a man. Men must think first, and then act to make manly and mature decisions. The more we make decisions based on emotion, the more childish we become.

This verse also shows us that a clear decision and action has to be made to grow up and put away childish things. Childish things are those things that are self-centered and benefit only self, sometimes at the expense of others.

There comes a time in each young man's life that he determines to be a man. When a boy decides to follow and demonstrate the manly attributes of Jesus, he decides to put away childish things and become a man.

The more we study the life of Jesus in the books of Matthew, Mark, Luke, & John, the more we can identify true manhood.

Manhood Key Point IV:

Manhood Can Sometime be A Dangerous Thing

Jesus is often portrayed in movies and in paintings as a weak, skinny, soft spoken, crying hippie with a lamb on his shoulders. Many churches portray Jesus as a timid, quiet, love-and-flowers kind of man. But that's not a true Biblical image of Jesus.

Jesus was a rugged, muscular, carpenter not only with physical strength, but also a force of character, and manly strength that had not previously been seen on the Earth. When Jesus spoke, he brought it strong and with confidence. So much so that people remarked and said "The people were amazed at his teaching, for he taught with real authority--quite unlike the teachers of religious law." (Mark 1:22)

He was no coward. He stood up to those who needed confronting, and *He even beat guys up in church.*

We read the account of this, in John Chapter 2: "Jesus made a whip from some ropes and chased them all out of the Temple. He drove out the sheep and cattle, scattered the moneychangers' coins over the floor, and turned over their tables. (John 2:15)

I also like the analogy of Jesus, made in the book "The Lion, The Witch and The Wardrobe" by C.S. Lewis. In this passage, Susan is asking Mr. Beaver about Aslan the Lion, an analogy of Jesus, whom they had not yet met:

"Mr. Beaver remarked, "Aslan is a lion- the Lion, the great Lion." "Ooh" said Susan. "I'd thought he was a man. Is he quite safe? I shall feel rather nervous about meeting a lion"..."Safe?" said Mr. Beaver..."Who said anything about safe? 'Course he isn't safe. But he's good. He's the King, I tell you."

As a man, you will need to stand up and confront evil with manly strength. This will mean that you might have to display a more aggressive side at times. While not advocating violence by any means, being a man is sometimes an edgy and dangerous thing. It's not timid, quiet, and weak. Popular culture would rather have men that are more feminine, because it seems safer. But you weren't created to be a woman, you weren't created to be an angel, you were created to be a man. And as a man, you are expected to exude manhood.

Mission:

Dad, prepare to tell your son one 'wrong' characteristic of manhood that you were taught as a young man and how you relearned the correct definition later in that area.

____

____

____

____

____

____

____

Dad, share with your son an example of Christ like manhood that you have seen demonstrated by a great man in your life.

____

____

____

____

____

____

____

LESSON 2

COURAGE

Courage

It was the fall season during my fifth grade year at Rutherford Elementary in Mesquite, TX. I lived directly across the field in a small brick home with my family. My Dad worked in construction and was not often at home. My mom worked as well, so I was left to fend for myself most of the time. I was considered a "latch-key kid."

My Dad was a rough and rugged bar fighter who liked to drink, fight, and party most nights.

He shared his fight stories with me, and I can remember feeling the adrenaline course through me as he shared heroic stories of fights during his youth against bullies.

I wanted to be tough like my dad. I wanted to be a hero like he was in my eyes.

During school one Friday, I had a run-in with the school bully, Scott. He was a grade older and a head taller. I don't remember doing anything to make him mad, but he sure was. Maybe I breathed his air or stepped on his part of the floor. I don't know. But he was going to kill me for whatever I did wrong.

He told me, in front of the entire 5th & 6th grade, "I'm going to pound you after school. I'll see you at the bike rack at 3:30."

That was the longest day of my life. I watched the clock. I tried to imagine how I might get out of this predicament. I even asked God to take me to heaven before 3:30. Nothing happened.

Finally, as the last 20 minutes of the class arrived, I went to Mrs. Owens's desk and told her, "My mom asked me to leave early today, I have to get home and help her." I flat out lied. I was desperate.

It was the only thing I could think of, to get out and away before Scott realized I was gone. Maybe he would forget over the weekend.

I gathered my stuff, headed out past the bike rack, into the field and started walking, my eyes fixed on the target of my house. Safety.

I walked 100 yards or so through the field and was halfway home. When I turned to see how far I was from danger, I thought I saw them.

Oh no, the entire school was following Scott out the doors and through the field after me. My pace quickened. I moved as quickly as I could without running toward my home and the safety of a locked door. I was just about to clear the field and step into the street separating the schoolyard from my front yard when I looked up and saw him.

My Dad was there sitting uncharacteristically on the front porch waiting for me to come home.

He's never home! Why now? What in the world is he doing on the porch? Then my mind began to reel. What will I tell him if he wonders why everyone in the free world is following me home today? Maybe he won't notice. Maybe I will make it to my room; the kids will see him and turn around, just maybe...

But he had already spotted the crowd.

As I tried to walk past him and into the house, I said without looking him in the eye, "Hi Dad, gotta get to my homework, see ya later..."

He reached out and barred my entrance to the house. "Whoa there. What's that all about?" He said as he nodded toward the fast approaching crowd.

I erupted in tears, "Dad, that kid is going to kill me. He's the toughest kid in our school and he wants to pound me. I can't fight him, I've got to get inside!"

My Dad's eyes narrowed in anger as he looked at me directly in the eyes. "You turn around and you get out there and you knock the stuffing out of that kid right now. If you don't I'm going to make you wish you had."

His words struck me. Where was the compassion? Where was the sympathy? Where was my mom?

I feared this man more than any Scott or anyone for that matter. I slowly turned and wheeled toward the crowd and walked slowly across the street where Scott and certain death awaited me. My eyes were filled with tears and I knew I was done.

As I stepped sheepishly toward Scott I could see that he had a bulge in his lip where a wad of snuff resided. Then he spit it right into my eyes! I was totally blinded and shocked by this act of cruelty. I ducked my head in rage, stepped forward toward where I remembered Scott to be and swung as hard as I could. I brought my fist all the way down from South Dallas all the way into Scott's snuff-filled mouth.

And I connected. By the time my right fist reached him, the left was right behind, another connection. Soon, my fists where wheeling rapid fire into Scott's face. He tipped backward and then down onto the hard dirt on his back. I lunged on top of him and mounted him for a steady rain of punches. I vowed I would not stop until next spring. I must have hit him 3 or 4 more times as he tried to cover his face and head, to no avail.

Then I felt a large hand grab me by the back of my pants inside my belt. The hand lifted me up off Scott and onto my feet a few paces away.

It was my Dad. He had come to save poor Scott. He told Scott and the rest of the shocked group, "It's over, get out of here. You've done enough and its over with."

He looked at Scott and told him, "You fought like a man and have nothing to be ashamed of. Tony kicked your tail and that's all there is to it. Let's end it here, shake hands and leave it alone, for good. Agreed?"

Scott looked at my Dad and looked at me. I was raring to get loose at him after realizing that he was now scared of me. Sensing this, he thrust out his hand and said. "OK, no hard feelings."

My Dad looked at me and winked, "Shake his hand, it's over."

I reached out and shook his hand and he never looked at me the same after that day. I never looked at myself the same. I had what it took. I would have never in a million years believed it. But my Dad made me face my fears and showed me that I had strength inside that I never knew.

Courage

"He who is brave is free" - Seneca

Four Key Points –

I. Courage Originates in the Heart.

II. Courage is the Mark of a Great Leader.

III. Courage is not the Absence of Fear.

IV. Being a Man Requires Courage

Key Verses:

I. *When they saw the courage of Peter and John and realized that they were unschooled, ordinary men, they were astonished and took note that these men had been with Jesus.* (Acts 4:13)

II. *For God has not given us a spirit of fear and timidity, but of power, love, and self-discipline.* (2 Timothy 1:7)

III. *The wicked run away when no one is chasing them, but the Godly are as bold as lions.* (Proverbs 28:1)

IV. *This is my command – be strong and courageous! Do not be afraid or discouraged. For the LORD your God is with you wherever you go.* (Joshua 1:9)

Courage Key Point I:

Courage begins in the heart.

The word courage comes from the Latin 'Cor" which, when translated to English, means heart. The word courage simply means having heart. Once we realize that our heart is the seat of courage, we begin examining the state of our heart. Is it plagued with fear or is it strong and full of courage?

Courage is the force that overcomes fear.

Courage is the force that tells us to move ahead when everything inside us is telling us to run away. Courage is the power that we summon to say "no" to fear and in spite of fear, respond in boldness, courage, and strength.

As a man, there will be many times when fear will grip you and try to stop you from doing the right thing. In all of these instances, you must try to respond with courage in spite of fear.

During these dangerous and crisis filled times, its time to kick our courage into the next gear. It's time to be men of courage. Our world and those around us desperately need men who are courageous and that inspire courage in others.

God continually commanded men throughout the Bible to take heart, or take courage.

The more we allow the Holy Spirit to fill our hearts, the more our hearts expand and the more courage we have.

I find it interesting in the bible that the same guy, Peter, who denied Jesus before a Junior High age girl, during the Book of Acts, stands up in front of a crowd exceeding 5,000 people and boldly confronts and commands them to repent for crucifying Jesus.

The difference in Peter from the first situation to the second is a personal encounter with and the largeness of heart given by the Holy Spirit. You may feel like the Peter who was intimidated by a little girl at times, or you may be ready to confront the 5,000, but we all need more courage to excel to be the men God created us to be.

When we spend time with Jesus, we become more courageous and our hearts enlarge. This is what happened to Jesus' disciples:

When they saw the courage of Peter and John and realized that they were unschooled, ordinary men, they were astonished and took note that these men had been with Jesus. (Acts 4:13)

The religious leaders of Jesus' day were amazed at his teaching because he didn't teach like everyone else. He taught with authority. In other words, He knew how to lay it straight. Where I come from in Texas, we'd say, "He knew how to shuck the corn." He could say with piercing conviction what needed to be said, even when it wasn't the popular thing to say. He had a huge heart. He had authority like no other because he had courage like no other.

Courage Key Point II:

Courage is the Mark of a Great Leader.

During the Egyptian campaign of the late 1700's, Napoleon Bonaparte was faced with a terrible dilemma. The bubonic plague was raging in Europe and specifically in one city Napoleon needed his troops to conquer. Because of fear of contracting the plague, his men were paralyzed and would not advance.

The plague was a horrible disease that killed millions. When one contracted the plague, they grew large knots beneath their arms and in other places. They developed large "buboles" which would swell and burst, as the powerless victim would die of raging fever, delirium, and pain.

To be in contact with the sick meant to catch the disease and die. Many would quarantine themselves from the sick, but it seemed to reach multitudes despite their precautions. Napoleon had an interesting theory that would help him to motivate his men to advance despite the danger; He knew it would take courage.

Napoleon is attributed as saying, "During the Egyptian campaign all those whose imagination was struck by fear died of it. The surest protection, the most efficacious remedy, was moral courage...The best way to preserve the army from the disease was to keep on the march and occupied. Diversion and fatigue were found to be the best prevention."

He did an amazing thing. He gathered his men together and walked down into the town. In full view of all the men, he picked up the corpse of a plague victim with busted buboles all over the body.

The story is told that he carried the corpse through his troops. While the stunned soldiers watched this act of complete disregard for danger, Napoleon carried the body close in his arms and announced that contact with the plague does not cause the plague, but fear of the plague causes it.

His amazed troops watched him over a period of days to see whether or not their leader would contract the deadly disease. To their surprise the leader remained fit, healthy, and full of vigor.

The men then came to the conclusion that fear was the cause of the plague, not control. They were spurred on by this act of courage to face their fears and advance.

Men follow other men who are courageous. You were created to be courageous, big in heart and a leader to be followed.

Face your fears and see the fears dissipate. The simple truth is - 99% of the things we fear never come to pass.

Courage Key Point III:

Courage is Not the Absence of Fear.

As the great cowboy actor John Wayne once said "Courage is being scared to death...and saddling up anyway."

Courage is not the absence of fear, but pushing ahead in spite of the fear to show courage and strength and not allowing fear to tell you what you *will* or *will not* do. A decision made out of fear will often lead to regret and an undesired outcome, long-term. A decision made from faith or courage will often result in a God sized outcome and bring contentment long-term.

Just because we get scared doesn't mean we are not courageous; it just means we are human. But what we do with that fear determines if we are courageous. If we let it control us, we are fearful. If we step up and face our fears, the death of fear is sure. Many of the brave and honorable things we have to do in life will be done with shaking knees and quivering voice. But we do them anyway.

I recently heard a statement from a psychologist indicating that we are only born with two innate fears: First, the fear of falling and secondly, the fear of loud noises. These fears can be healthy in helping us avoid danger and may even save our lives. All other fears are learned behaviors. But as we go through life, we can become afraid of different things and situations if we are not careful to guard our heart and refuse to allow fear to grip us.

Dr. Martin Luther King Jr. was a courageous leader in the civil rights movement and was arrested multiple times for his courageous stand against tyranny and injustice.

Courage Key Point IV:

Being a Man Requires Courage

Courage is the mark of a man and the more effective and powerful a man would seek to be, the more courage he will need.

As a man, it takes courage to:

- *Face reality* – Courageous men are able to realistically assess their situation and accept facts for what they are.
- *Admit need* – A courageous man is brave and humble enough to admit when he is in need and unable to make it by himself.
- *Change* - change is inevitable and will be a constant in life. It takes real courage to be able to adapt and make changes in a turbulent environment.
- *Make decisions* – decisiveness is the mark of a man. It was once said "not everyone likes strong leadership, but everyone hates weak leadership."
- *Hold convictions* – the sway of public opinion will rise and fall, but a man of courage has the inner strength to stand up when everyone around him is bowing.

It is inevitable that, as a man, you will be placed in situations where fear may try to grip you. Your preparation in this study will help you remember that fear is normal and can be overcome with courage.

Mission:

Dad: Think of and share a time when you were really afraid. Describe it to your son. Be sure to let him in on what you were thinking during this time, as it will help to identify his own thoughts. Next, tell him how you overcame that fear and what the outcome was. Give as much detail as possible. Then listen with patience and without giving advice or making judgment, as your son shares his biggest fears with you.

____

____

____

____

____

____

____

____

Son: Share with your Dad the biggest areas of fear in your life. Hold nothing back.

____

____

____

____

____

____

____

____

____

____

Teamwork: As a father & son team, discuss steps that you can take together to help overcome those fears.

Pray this prayer together out loud:

"Father, I thank you that you created me to be fearless. Help me to recognize that fear is not from you and to fight it with courage. Help me to be bold and to live every day as a courageous man."

LESSON 3

MATURITY

Maturity

There was an Asian monk living in a little remote village, tending his garden, spending much of his time in prayer. And then one day, he thought he heard the voice of God telling him to go to Rome.

The Monk obeyed the Lord's command and set out on foot toward Rome. Many weary weeks late, he arrived in the capital city of the Roman Empire at the time of a great festival that was going on in Rome. The little Monk followed the crowd that was surging down the streets into the Coliseum. He saw the gladiators come forth, stand before the Emperor, and say, "We who are about to die salute you." And, then, he realized these men were going to fight to the death for the entertainment of the crowd. The Monk cried out, "In the name of Christ, stop!"

And as the games began, he fought his way down through the crowd, climbed over the wall and dropped to the floor of the arena. When the crowd saw this tiny figure making his way out to the gladiators, saying, "In the name of Christ, stop," they thought it was part of the entertainment. They began laughing. But when they realized it wasn't, their laughter turned to anger. As the Monk was pleading with the gladiators to stop, one of them plunged a sword into his body, and he fell to the sand of the arena. As he was dying, his last words were, "In the name of Christ, stop." Then a strange thing began to happen. The gladiators stood looking at the tiny figure lying there in the sand. A hush fell over the Coliseum. Way up in the upper tiers, a man stood and made his way to the exit. Others began to follow. In dead silence, everyone left the Coliseum. And that was the last battle to the death between gladiators in the Roman Coliseum. Never again in the great stadium did men kill each other for the entertainment of the crowd. All because of one tiny voice that could hardly be heard above the tumult - one voice that spoke the truth in God's name.

(A story told by Ronald Reagan)

Maturity

"...But when I became a man, I put away childish things. "
– Paul of Tarsus

Four Key Points:

I. Maturity Doesn't Come with Age, but With the Acceptance of Responsibility.

II. Maturity Happens Outside the Comfort Zone

III. Accepting Responsibility is the First Step in Authentic Manhood.

IV. Responsibility is Demonstrated by our Response to Adversity

Four Key Verses:

I. *When I was a child, I spoke and thought and reasoned as a child. But when I grew up, I put away childish things.* (1 Corinthians 13:11)

II. *Until we all attain to the unity of the faith and of the knowledge of the Son of God, to mature manhood, to the measure of the stature of the fullness of Christ,* (Ephesians 4:13 ESV)

III. *He has made us a Kingdom of priests for God his Father. All glory and power to him forever and ever! Amen.* (Rev 1:6)

IV. *Rather, speaking the truth in love, we are to grow up in every way into him who is the head, into Christ,* (Ephesians 4:15 ESV)

Maturity Point I:

Maturity Doesn't Come With Age, But With The Acceptance of Responsibility

We all know someone who, though they are older in years, still remains immature. This effectively demonstrates the principle that you can grow old, but sometimes not grow up. Maturity doesn't happen because we age, it happens because we purpose to mature.

The Peter Pan Syndrome

In the favorite Disney cartoon Peter Pan, we are introduced to Peter, an older boy, who is perhaps much older that he appears. Peter lives in Never Ever Land where no one ages, no one takes responsibility, and there are no consequences.

Sadly, many men try to do the same thing. They try to hold onto their lives as children where they can live carefree and frivolous. They live for the charge and excitement of pleasure, games, and self-indulgence. The only problem with this plan is that there is no such thing as Never Ever Land. Life continues to progress and demand action with or without our readiness to handle it. Life is too precious, too holy, and too short for us to live in immaturity. You *can* choose *not* to grow up.

Response Plus Ability Equals Responsibility

The difference between boyhood and manhood is maturity. Even though a 5-year-old indicated that he would like to become a policeman when he grew up, we would never give him a loaded gun and badge right away. Why? *Because a 5 year old is not mature enough to handle the responsibilities of a police officer.* Responsibility is simply someone's response to his or her ability. As we respond to our ability, we go through the process of maturity and we grow up. When a boy initiates this response, he starts to grow up. If a boy has the ability to clean his room, mow the yard, take out the trash, or do other tasks required of him, and responds by doing it, he shows maturity. If he starts to do it without being asked, he demonstrates great responsibility and grows up quickly.

Maturity Point II:

Maturity Happens Outside the Comfort Zone

When you came out of your mother's womb, you left a warm, comfortable, safe place, no doubt screaming and crying into a cold, bright, loud, and scary environment. We all love comfort and safety and don't want to leave. But you quickly adapted and overcame. You toughened up and passed a threshold of resistance that made you stronger and more resilient. The process of maturity is no different. We must expand and push out into more unsure and hostile environments to become really mature and ready for manhood.

When an Eagle builds its nest, it builds with the process of maturity in mind. The Eagle begins the nest with thorn branches, barbed and coarse wood, sharp rocks, and even pieces of glass. Over this rough and uncomfortable framework, the Eagle lays in yarn, fabric, and soft down feathers to keep the baby eagles warm, comfortable, and protected. But as the chick begins to grow and the nest becomes too small, the mother Eagle begins to remove the soft nesting material to reveal a sharp and uncomfortable frame. The baby eagle is forced to leave the nest and become a strong flyer. Similarly, we grow into our environment. But often, it is not a comfortable process. This helps us push out and soar in more majestic environments.

There was a certain young man who dove for a living, capturing exotic fish for aquariums. The young man told us that the most popular fish he was asked to capture was the shark. He said that sharks, like many fish, grow in proportion to the environment in which they live. He also said that if you can catch a baby shark and put it into a small aquarium, it would not grow much. You might be able to have a full grown shark that was only 6 inches long, where if it had been in the ocean, would have become over ten feet long. The same is true of men. When we step into larger responsibility, we become larger inside and more mature. We must become mature because those around us need us to be mature.

Maturity Point III:

Accepting responsibility is the First Step in Authentic Manhood

The Apostle Paul told his spiritual sons about the first step to becoming a man when he shared his own entrance into manhood by saying:

> "When I was a child, I spoke and thought and reasoned as a child. But when I grew up, I put away childish things. (1 Corinthians 13:11)

Note that he took the initiative to put away the things that he determined were childish. What are those childish things? For most men, the same childish things apply.

- Being the center of Your own universe
- Demanding Your own way
- Selfishness
- Temper tantrums
- Seeking to please yourself at the expense of others.

- Illogical and unable to be reasoned with.
- Moody and easily angered.

Also, note that the description of a child involves speaking first, then thinking, then reasoning. Manhood is quite different. Men first think and reason, then speak. Children feel, then act while men act, then feel. Children react while men respond.

Maturity Point IV:

Responsibility is Demonstrated by our Response to Adversity

When a man responds to adversity with strength, poise, and determination, he demonstrates his maturity. The less mature we are, the more things "rattle our cage."

Good Timber

The tree that never had to fight

For sun and sky and air and light,

That stood out in the open plain

And always got its share of rain,

Never became a forest king

But lived and died a scrubby thing.

The man who never had to toil

To heaven from the common soil,

Who never had to win his share

Of sun and sky and light and air,

Never became a manly man,

But lived and died as he began.

Good timber does not grow in ease;

The stronger wind, the tougher trees;

The farther sky, the greater length;

The more the storm, the more the strength;

By sun and cold, by rain and snows,

In tree or man, good timber grows.

Where thickest stands the forest growth

We find the patriarchs of them both;

And they hold converse with the stars

Whose broken branches show the scars

Of many winds and of much strife —   This is the

common law of life.

(Douglas Malloch)

It is not in the vacuum of a soft and comfortable life that authentic masculinity and manhood is formed. Often it is the crucible of adversity. The toughest of times have produced the Lion's share of strong men. Knowing this, we can understand that adversity can help us to demonstrate our maturity and strength. Resistance is what is needed to build bulging biceps.

Our nature is to enjoy relaxation and ease, but that doesn't build strength. We have to allow adversity to have its work and push ourselves sometimes out in the storm to experience a challenge to our manly strength.

When my son was very young, but beginning to show signs of wanting to wrestle and play, I would move our furniture in the living room back, we would take off our shirts and have epic wrestling battles. As he became stronger, I would give him more resistance, more of a fight.

I can remember his mother crying out from the kitchen for me to stop wrestling him, for fear that he would be hurt. I would explain to her that this is what makes boys men. I would let him display his desire to fight and wrestle. Those battles we shared prepared him as he played football, and interacted with his peers. It taught him to be strong, manly, and aggressive. This is something his mother couldn't understand. I used to tell her, "Trust me, I know how to make a man."

Daniel became a strong man and remembers fondly our epic battles on the living room floor.

Mothers can teach spirituality, but only a man can pass the torch of masculinity.

A group of tourists asked an old man if any great men were born in the small town they were visiting. He replied "No, only babies."

Mission:

Dads:

Explain to your son some key areas that you have to care for others (could be by working to provide for your family, or serving in the military or another instance where you have had to sacrifice for others.)

I have to demonstrate maturity by taking responsibility for others in these areas:

____

____

____

____

Sons:

Ask your Dad for one area that he can identify where you can become more responsible.

____

____

____

____

Teamwork:

As a team, find a way to bless mom by being more responsible around the home. Maybe plan a day where you send mom to get a manicure/pedicure or spa day. If that's not possible, arrange for her to spend the day with a friend or family member while you both clean the house, prepare a dinner, provide fresh flowers, make her a card and make a special evening for her.

Pray this Together:

"Father, thank you for helping us be the men that you created us to be by expressing our maturity and responsibility. Help us become better men by helping us identify areas where we can be more responsible."

LESSON 4

LEADERSHIP

Leadership

The following story was written by Michael Rogers, in his leadership blog:

"The Civil War was a bloody and vicious war. At least 618,000 Americans died and some say the toll reached 700,000. Casualties exceeded all of America's other wars from the Revolution through Vietnam.

In the winter of 1862, General Robert E. Lee's forces had claimed several key battlefields in the Eastern Campaign. One of those key battles was as one-sided a victory as a battle could be. It was the Battle of Fredericksburg.

On December 13, 1862, Union forces began what was termed a desperate and eventual doomed assault on a heavily fortified position known as the "stone wall at the sunken road."

After crossing a river, the Union confidentially took the town of Fredericksburg with little resistance. The confederate army had voluntarily given up the town so that they might fortify themselves along a stone wall at the base of a sloping hill. As the Union Army began to approach the wall, they were attacked and by the morning of December 14th over 8,000 Union soldiers had been shot in front of the stone wall. Many of those remaining on the battlefield were still alive, but suffering from their wounds, the cold and thirst.

During that night, both sides were forced to listen to the cries and moans of those soldiers for hours. A Confederate soldier stationed near the wall later stated that it was "weird, unearthly, terrible to hear and bear the cries of dying soldiers filling the air – lying crippled on a hillside so many miles from home – breaking the hearts of soldiers on both sides of the battlefield."

Richard Rowland Kirkland, an infantry sergeant for the Confederacy could not rest or sleep due to the suffering of the Union soldiers and that morning asked his commanding officer if he could scale the wall and provide water for the suffering Union troops. The commanding officer was reluctant at first because of the danger to Richard, but later allowed him to. As Richard climbed the wall several shots were instantly fired thinking that Kirkland's motives were to wound more, but after realizing what was happening shooting ceased. Richard Rowland Kirkland made his way to each soldier comforting them the best he could by laying his jacket over one and providing water to the thirsty lips of all. For the next hour and a half, he would scale the wall a number of times with his canteen to get more water for his enemy. It was a moment that temporarily stopped the Civil War."

This story deeply touched me. To me, this exemplifies the highest calling of leadership. And it embodies the purpose of leadership. That purpose is to care and to serve. Is there one man on that battlefield that wouldn't have been willing to follow such a servant if asked to? He was the enemy of course, but how much more powerful the example."

Leadership

"*If your actions inspire others to dream more, learn more, do more and become more, you are a leader.*"

-John Quincy Adams

Four Key Points:

I. Leaders are Necessary

II. Leadership is a Decision

III. Leaders Must Have Vision

IV. True Leadership is Service

Four Key Verses:

I. *And you should imitate me, just as I imitate Christ.* (1 Corinthians 11:1)

II. *The greatest among you must be a servant.* (Matthew 23:11)

III. *And if it seem evil unto you to serve the LORD, choose you this day whom ye will serve;* (Joshua 24:15 KJV)

IV. *Where there is no vision, the people perish: but he that keepeth the law, happy is he.* (Proverbs 29:18 KJV)

Leadership Point I:

Leaders are Necessary

Peter Drucker once said, ""The only things that evolve by themselves in an organization are disorder, friction, and under-performance. Everything else requires leadership to develop."

Each time I hold a leadership teaching, I begin with a very revealing activity about leadership. I instruct the participants to close their eyes tightly and promise not to open them and look during the activity. I then instruct them to, without looking, point in the direction that they think is north. I remind them again, "no peeking."

After everyone is sure of their choice for north, I instruct them to open their eyes and look. Almost every hand is pointed in a different direction.

Leaders point North. In organizations of all sorts, a leader always points the correct direction for that organization. Without them, we all have an idea of the direction we should go, but it's up to the leader to point the way. Every organization, including a family, needs a leader.

Leadership Point II:

Leadership is A Decision

Each year, during the spring, we hold "Men of Honor" camps for young men. We begin leadership training almost immediately by taking the young men through exercises that help them think about their leadership ability.

The first exercise they participate in begins the second they arrive at the camp. A leader steps onto the bus in which they just arrived and in a voice reminiscent of boot camp shouts out, "without talking, everybody get off the bus and immediately circle up in groups of 3 or 4, facing each other in a circle. Quickly, circle up and – no talking."

The young men are still unsure of what's going on, but they quickly form up in circles of three or four, facing each other silently.

Then the leader shouts out, "Sit down when you KNOW you're NOT the leader. Quickly sit down when you KNOW you're NOT the leader."

An interesting phenomenon begins to take place. Some of the young men sit down immediately while others look around and watch what the others are doing before sitting down. Sometimes we end up with two guys looking at each other, each gesturing to the boy across to sit down.

At the end of the exercise, we end up with one young man standing in each circle, while the others are seated on the ground.

At that point, I step forward and ask those seated, "Why did you give it up? Why couldn't you be the leader?"

The responses begin with, "He's older." or "He's bigger," or a myriad other reasons why they didn't remain standing.

At that point, I begin to teach these young men that leadership is always a decision. We choose to stand up or sit down in every situation. Leadership is always a choice. After this exercise, every time I ask, "Who is the leader here?" Every single hand will rise.

Leaders Should Lead

From the very beginning, God gave mankind a charge. He told man to "take dominion."

This simple charge is the same for men today. God wants us to take dominion. Another way of saying it is "rule over our domain". You might have a huge domain of business, ministry, or very little to rule. Regardless, God's expectation for you is that you would rule it well or *take dominion.*

Dr. Edwin Louis Cole described this process of dominion to mean that we "guide, guard, and govern" the domain God has given us.

The problem with most men is that they refuse to lead. And as a result, like Adam, bad stuff ends up slithering into our domains. Leaders must be people of action who make decisions and take responsibility for their domains.

It might be as simple as making sure that your bedroom is clean, your homework is done, and your relationships with your family are strong and on a good path.

If something is wrong, a leader stops and makes corrective action. Clean the room, do the homework, reach out to that person and make things right, right now. That's what leaders do; they take the initiative to make things happen. They don't wait for someone else to lead; they take the lead in every situation.

We have a saying that we teach our boys that helps them to remember that they have the power to lead. It very simply states, "If there is no man, I will be the man.

Because you are a man, you were created to be a leader. The world needs you to lead. Those around you need you to lead. Great things happen when God's men lead.

"God-given dreams in a God-favored man, make a God-blessed world." – Ed Cole

To be effective leaders, we start right where we are with the responsibilities we were given and lead those well. When those have been led well, we will find ourselves being promoted to higher levels of leadership. But we start right where we are, and lead well.

Leadership Point III:

Leaders Must Have Vision

In the early days of the westward expansion of the United States that took place during the 1800's, pioneers left their homes on the East Coast in search of fortune out West. They put their belongings, families, and dreams in wagons and headed across rugged and dangerous terrain. They would face many obstacles on their journeys. At the head of each wagon train there were scouts that went ahead and lead the wagon train. The scout rode ahead and scouted the route, identified the danger, and prepared the wagons for the obstacles that lay ahead.

The scout had to see forward and have vision for the horizon. He had to identify dangers, opportunities, and be prepared for them. In the same way, as men, we must live with vision.

Having vision for those around us is a critical component of manhood. When we have vision, we can effectively lead the way. No one wants to follow someone who is lost; they all want to follow someone who has a plan, someone who knows the way.

Components of vision include:

- Knowing where you are – "What's the current state of our situation?"

- Knowing what the obstacles are – potential hindrances to forward progress.

- Knowing what the potential is – seeing the best in others.

- Knowing the goal – "where are we going?"

During the 1960's the U.S. was in tense relationship with the Soviet Union. We came dangerously close to world war with the Soviets and were in a technology race to establish dominance in the world. If the Soviets thought that they were superior in arms and technology, America could be at risk of invasion.

Seeing the dangers and needing a strong show of American technology and arms capability, then President John F. Kennedy saw and communicated a vision to the United States that would energize and unite Americans to a display of force that had never been seen in the world. We would do the impossible. We would "put a man on the moon."

President Kennedy's vision for what was needed and ability to communicate the vision caused the U.S. to rise to the challenge to dominate the space race and ensure America's place of technological dominance over the Soviets in the last century.

Leadership Point IV:

True Leadership is Service

If you research the topic of leadership in the current body of knowledge and popular culture, you will find an unending stream of information, self-help, and resources on leadership. However, if you look for the subject of service and servant-hood, the list is much smaller. The world's perspective on leadership can be summed up as "making people do what you want them to do to accomplish your goal as a leader". Jesus introduced a revolutionary concept of leadership that is contrary to modern leadership philosophy. Jesus introduced the principle that the servant is actually the leader. When a man serves and helps those around him, he qualifies himself as the leader. Ed Cole so aptly stated that, "You are qualified to lead to the extent you are willing to serve." Jesus taught us that the greatest would be the servant of all. Although counter-intuitive, when a man causes another to serve him, he actually makes them the leader. True leadership is service.

Mission:

Dads: Prepare and share a time when you were given your first responsibilities. What did that look like? What was your experience? Note: Share the positive and negatives. Feel free to share a time when you failed. It will help your son or grandson to see your transparency and identify areas where he can avoid failure.

____

____

____

____

____

Son: Identify 2 areas that God has given you as your domain.

____

____

____

____

____

____

Also, ask your Dad for advice on how to better lead in those two areas.

Teamwork:

As a team, list three areas each that God has given you dominion.

____

____

____

____

____

In what areas of these domains do you see things that need to be made right?

Pray this prayer:

"Lord, thank you that you created me to be a leader. As Father & son, help us to identify areas that we can demonstrate our leadership better. Help us to become the leaders you created us to be. In Jesus Name, Amen."

LESSON 5

DILIGENCE

Diligence

"I *'d hold you up to say to your mother, "this kid's gonna be the best kid in the world. This kid's gonna be somebody better than anybody I ever knew." And you grew up good and wonderful. It was great just watching you, every day was like a privilege. Then the time comes for you to be your own man and take on the world, and you did. But somewhere along the line, you changed. You stopped being you. You let people stick a finger in your face and tell you you're no good. And when things got hard, you started looking for something to blame, like a big shadow.*

Let me tell you something you already know. The world ain't all sunshine and rainbows. It's a very mean and nasty place and I don't care how tough you are it will beat you to your knees and keep you there permanently if you let it. You, me, or nobody is gonna hit as hard as life. But it ain't about how hard you hit. It's about how hard you can get hit and keep moving forward. How much you can take and keep moving forward.

That's how winning is done! Now if you know what you're worth then go out and get what you're worth. But ya gotta be willing to take the hits, and not pointing fingers saying you ain't where you wanna be because of him, or her, or anybody! Cowards do that and that ain't you! You're better than that! I'm always gonna love you no matter what. No matter what happens. You're my son and you're my blood. You're the best thing in my life. But until you start believing in yourself, ya ain't gonna have a life."

– From the Character Rocky Balboa- Rocky Balboa – The Final Fight 2006

Diligence

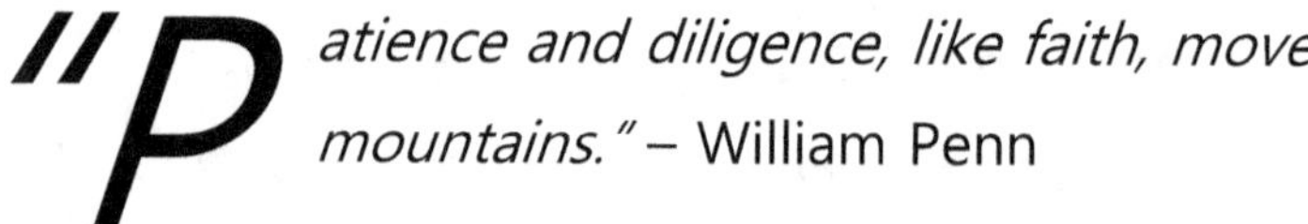

"Patience and diligence, like faith, move mountains." – William Penn

Four Key Points:

I. The Diligent are Never Mediocre

II. Diligence is Evidence of an Excellent Spirit

III. Diligence adds Extra to the Ordinary and Makes You Extraordinary

IV. Diligence allows us to do now What Cannot be Done Later

Four Key Verses:

I. *Work hard and become a leader; be lazy and become a slave.* (Proverbs 12:24)

II. *Do your diligence to come before winter.* (2 Timothy 4:21 KJV 2000)

III. *Don't brag about tomorrow, since you don't know what the day will bring.* (Proverbs 27:1)

IV. *Do you see any truly competent workers? They will serve kings rather than working for ordinary people.* (Proverbs 22:29)

Scientists tell us that genetically and anatomically, we are 99% similar to every person living on the planet right now. That means you and I are just like 6 billion people currently living on the planet. But our 1% can make us as drastically different and special as anyone else on the planet. The greater our 1% can be, is contingent on our diligence. Diligence can make your 1% either spectacular or mediocre.

Diligence Point I:

The Diligent are Never Mediocre

Each year, one of the popular climbs in Colorado has hordes of climbing enthusiasts who wish to climb its lofty peak. They begin the arduous journey up a trail that will lead them to a panoramic view at the top of the snow-capped mountain. Those committed climbers who make it to the top will experience a beautiful, rewarding, and rare glimpse of creation. That coupled with the sense of accomplishment that such a hike brings, attracts thousands annually.

The air is thin, the trail is steep, and the journey is not easy.

At the midway point, there is a chalet where a warm fireplace, a place to sit and rest, and a large mug of hot chocolate are available to each climber. The group stops and rests for a short period before returning to the thin air, burning leg muscles, and forced determination of the climb.

But many of the climbers decide that the respite of the chalet will suffice for their summit. They decide to stay and relax while the others continue the climb without them. They bid them good luck and tell them they will be waiting for them when they return after the summit.

The determined climbers leave the chalet and those resting enjoy the warmth, the hot chocolate, and conversation of their fellow relaxing team.

But, the chalet has a feature that the resting group is not yet aware of. There is a bell that rings each time a group reaches the summit of the mountain, several thousand feet above, announcing that the group that kept going has reached the top. As the bell rings, the conversation stops, and a hushed silence falls on the group. A sense of disappointment and regret fills the group. Many begin to voice their regret, "I wish I would have kept going..."

How many men live their lives full of regrets, because they refused to persevere? Keep going!

This is your chance to re-ignite the passion of your heart and launch your life onto a new path of greatness. You were not meant to be mediocre.

The word mediocre means just what this story illustrates; "Medi" from the Latin word medius, which means middle or halfway. And "ocre" from the Latin ocrus, which is a word for mountain.

Mediocre means "half way up the mountain".

It is Newton's law of motion, a dynamic force that guides the principle - A body in motion, tends to stay in motion.

In order to break the pull of a mediocre life, you've got to break the orbit of past, failure, and mediocrity. Once in motion you become an unstoppable force to be used by God to change your world. You were not created to fail, but you were created to win.

When you were conceived, there were 1 million or more little swimmers each contending for the prize. They were all endowed with a desire to win and the tools to get them there. But you were the champion. You were the one that broke through victorious. You were created for victory. At conception, you were already declared a winner. God always causes us to triumph, as his word says:

"Now thanks be unto God, which always causeth us to triumph in Christ, and maketh manifest the savour of his knowledge by us in every place." (2 Corinthians 2:14)

You cannot believe the lies that the enemy says about who you are, you must believe what God says about you; you are a mighty man of God.

One of the strongest displays of diligence, honor, vigilance and an excellent spirit is the Guard of the Tomb of the Unknown Soldier.

These elite members of the special guard are on duty at the tomb of the unknown, where lies entombed, the remains of an unknown soldier from battle. This tomb represents the honor due to those who laid down their lives in defense of their country and because they were unable to be identified, were unable to be interred by family and friends.

As a result, these special soldiers deserve and receive the highest honor our country provides. The guard for this tomb is on duty 7 days a week, 24 hours a day, in an eternal and vigilant display of respect and honor. The members of the guard are chosen and give their duties uncommon diligence.

The guards of The Tomb have a long-standing tradition. Every time they salute an officer at the tomb they say, "Line six sir!" This saying is a reference to line six of the 99 word "Sentinel's Creed". The creed they are sworn to uphold as part of this elite corps of "Guards of the Unknown."

Their Creed says:

"My dedication to this sacred duty is total and whole-hearted. In the responsibility bestowed on me never will I falter. And with dignity and perseverance my standard will remain perfection. Through the years of diligence and praise and the discomfort of the elements, I will walk my tour in humble reverence to the best of my ability. It is he who commands the respect I protect, his bravery that made us so proud. Surrounded by well meaning crowds by day, alone in the thoughtful peace of night, this soldier will in honored glory rest under my eternal vigilance."

Tomb of the Unknown – Arlington National Cemetery

Diligence Point II:

Diligence Displays a Spirit of Excellence

When Daniel was just a child, the Babylonians invaded his land. Daniel was captured by the invading army and taken to a foreign land. Daniel was plunged into a foreign world where everyone spoke a different language. His entire world was turned upside down.

Though his situation was dark, Daniel always looked to the light of God's presence to illuminate his heart and mind. Each day he would seek encouragement and strength to face the strange world into which he was unwillingly thrust. Each night he would pray for comfort and deliverance.

Daniel was placed in the home of Ashpenaz, the King of Babylon's chief of staff. They changed Daniel's name to Belteshazzar, and began to teach him the language and literature of the Babylonians. Under this training, Daniel began to flourish. Because his hope was in God, God's hand was upon him. He grew each day in wisdom, stature, and favor.

Each day they would bring him rich food and wine from the Kings table. Each day, he would refuse and eat only the vegetables and drink water and the foods he was accustomed to from home. He held to his diligence in diet and belief that the foods God had commanded him to eat were the only foods he would eat, regardless of the commands of a King. He set his heart not to defile himself.

Each time he was brought before the King to give his opinion on a matter, they found him to be ten times more capable than the wise men of Babylon.

Diligence brings promotion.

Daniel was a man of diligence regardless of the situations and circumstances around him.

Those around Daniel became jealous and bitter as they watched him rise in favor to the very top. The only way they would be able to bring him down was to try and make his virtue a fault.

Using the King's own vanity and pride, they tricked him into making a law that stated "anyone caught praying to any God besides the King" would be executed immediately.

This would be a problem for Daniel, as he prayed to the LORD five times a day.

But Daniel would not stop praying. He was a man of diligence, even if it cost him everything. The outcome of this story was that even though he was caught praying and sentenced to death, God delivered Daniel and caused the entire Kingdom to know that only the one true God was to be worshipped. And Daniel was his main man. He would be promoted and those that sought to destroy him would be killed instead. Daniel would then be promoted to a higher level of esteem, favor, and influence. In his lifetime, he affected 5 world leaders by his example of Godly diligence.

Diligence Point III:

Diligence adds Extra to the Ordinary and Makes You Extraordinary

Vince Lombardi was considered by many to be one of the winningest Coaches of all time. He was inducted into the NFL hall of fame and the NFL's championship trophy was named after him.

1958, the year before Vince Lombardi became coach of the Green Bay Packers, was the worst year in Packer history. Their record was 1-10-1. Coach Lombardi went to work and created a training regiment that was the toughest in the league. His philosophy was that the team that was in the best shape, played the hardest, and gave their best effort would win-every time. The team immediately improved. So much so, that Lombardi was named NFL Coach of the Year. The fans immediately responded to the improvements and the team sold out Lambeau field for every pre-season, regular season and playoff game and have done so every single year, for the last 44 years. The Packers went on to win championships and Super Bowls. Vince Lombardi took an ordinary team and asked them to give a little extra. The result was – they became extraordinary. This was in large part due to Coach Lombardi's insistence on preparation, diligence, and a strong second effort, every time. He would say things like: *"The difference between a successful person and others is not a lack of strength, not a lack of knowledge, but rather a lack of will." And also, "Winning is not a sometime thing; it's an all the time thing. You don't win once in a while; you don't do things right once in a while; you do them right all of the time. Winning is a habit.*

Unfortunately, so is losing. There is no room for second place. There is only one place in my game, and that's first place. I have finished second twice in my time at Green Bay, and I don't ever want to finish second again. There is a second place bowl game, but it is a game for losers played by losers. It is and always has been an American zeal to be first in anything we do, and to win, and to win, and to win."

He would require 100% commitment from his team. He said, "Every time a football player goes to play his trade he's got to play from the ground up - from the soles of his feet right up to his head. Every inch of him has to play. Some guys play with their heads. That's O.K. You've got to be smart to be number one in any business. But more importantly, you've got to play with your heart, with every fiber of your body. If you're lucky enough to find a guy with a lot of head and a lot of heart, he's never going to come off the field second."

Running a football team is no different than running any other kind of organization - an army, a political party or a business. The principles are the same. The object is to win - to beat the other guy. Maybe that sounds hard or cruel. I don't think it is.

It is a reality of life that men are competitive and the most competitive games draw the most competitive men. That's why they are there - to compete. The object is to win fairly, squarely, by the rules - but to win.

And in truth, I've never known a man worth his salt who in the long run, deep down in his heart, didn't appreciate the grind, the discipline. There is something in good men that really yearns for discipline and the harsh reality of head to head combat.

I don't say these things because I believe in the 'brute' nature of men or that men must be brutalized to be combative. I believe in God, and I believe in human decency. But I firmly believe that any man's finest hour -- his greatest fulfillment to all he holds dear -- is that moment when he has worked his heart out in a good cause and lies exhausted on the field of battle - victorious."

- Coach Vincent T. Lombardi

Jesus told his disciples that they should always, "go the extra mile." It's never crowded in the extra mile, because very few choose to distinguish themselves by going above what is expected. But in the extra mile is where champions are made and excellence is displayed.

Diligence Point IV:

Diligence Allows us to do Now What Cannot be Done Later

The Apostle Paul told Timothy to 'do his diligence to come to me before winter". He told him to come because he knew that if he waited 'til winter, the trade routes in the sea and ancient navigation conditions would not allow him to arrive until Spring, in which case, Paul would already be dead. The point here being, the things we can do now, we should do. Because the time will come when we will be unable to do them.

Men of Diligence listen and respond when people come with a need. They handle it right then and there. In life, there are often no second chances given when opportunity knocks. That is why it is important to do what we can do, while we can.

Complete the task before you with excellence. Each task that comes before you requires the judgment of whether it is worthy of your efforts. If it is worthy of your efforts, it must be given your very best effort.

Whatever you do, work at it with all your heart, as working for the Lord, not for human masters, (Colossians 3:23 NIV)

Mission:

Dads, prepare to share a time when you either capitalized or missed an opportunity because of diligence.

____

____

____

Sons, identify three key areas that you need to show more diligence in and ask your Dad to pray for you in those areas.

____

____

____

Teamwork:

Fathers, help your sons to develop a daily checklist or to do list that will help him be more diligent in the key areas he has identified as needing help.

Pray this:

"Father, help me to be more diligent and excellent in spirit than I have ever been before. Help me to identify and stay consistent in the areas that you have shown me. In Jesus name, Amen."

LESSON 6

STRENGTH

Strength

I was recently at the gym with my son Daniel. It was a Sunday evening and I had just finished a weekend retreat for men, and I was exhausted. We lifted for a while and Daniel indicated that he wanted to go and play basketball on the courts there. I told him to go ahead, I was going to the sauna to relax. As I entered the small sauna, I entered a room jam packed with shoulder-to-shoulder sweating men. I grunted, pointed toward a thin spot between two large men, ducked my head, and moved forward, refusing to be denied a seat. They both quickly moved aside and let me sit down. I relaxed, closed my eyes, and took in the heat and steamy air.

After a few minutes, a young man entered the sauna carrying two dumbbells. He was tatted up, had huge muscled arms, designs shaved in his head, and a crazy look in his eyes. I glanced up once, but quickly closed my eyes again. The young man, about 25, didn't sit down like everyone else, but stood in the middle of the small room facing us all on the benches.....very awkward.

He began curling the two dumbbells and telling stories as though someone had asked, "What'd *you* do this weekend?" But the funny thing was, no one had said anything. He began to tell of his bravado and physical prowess and how he had unmercifully beat a guy who dared to challenge him. Every other word out of his mouth was an expletive. I mean really foul language. When he finished one story of a fight, he began another. Each story portrayed himself victorious over an opponent.

After a few minutes, one, then two guys got up and left the sauna. It was getting increasingly tense.

The young man continued to curl the dumbbells. As the heat of the sauna and the effort of the exercise peaked, this guy began to sweat profusely and swear more. He seemed to be working himself into some sort of angry frenzy. This time he was facing me, and each curl slung his sweat right into my face. It's like the sweat had singled me out.

Suddenly I heard something in my heart say, "Are you going to sit here quietly, or are you going to say something?"

I thought for a moment and then answered that familiar voice in my heart. "Yes Lord, I'm going to say something..."

After a few seconds gathering my thoughts, I sat up, opened my eyes, and looked into his. Then with a voice that caused everyone to turn toward me I said..."You know what your problem is?"

Another guy eased up off the bench and left the sauna.

The young man looked at me with a sinister look and said, "No, what's that?"

I took a moment and said, "You are a warrior and you were made to be strong.....but you don't have a battle to fight."

He looked around at everyone in the sauna and began curling the weights again, this time a little slower. After a few minutes of awkward silence, he started up again and began telling other stories. He would look up at me, from time-to-time trying to figure out what my comment really meant. Then, after a few more minutes of prayer to myself, I *really* moved in. "Tell me about your Dad." This is the quickest way for me to get to the heart of a man. It reveals such a place of deep emotion for all men, especially those who are wounded by the absence of a father.

He looked at me and began to unravel a story about his childhood in Bosnia, his father abandoning him and his brother; war, civil war, killing in the streets and unbelievable pain. I began to feel the father heart of God aching for this wounded young man.

It was then that I noticed he was wearing an ankle monitor. He told me that he had been out of jail for a month, that he had been a severe alcoholic, and that he was celebrating his first two weeks of being sober. I told him something that a father had probably never told him. "I'm proud of you..."

His voice and demeanor began to soften and I began to feel a love for this wounded young man. He shared how his greatest struggle had been his inability to find work. I told him that I would pray for him. He thanked me as though he thought it was an empty gesture, but I meant that I was going to pray for him...*right now.* I stood, reached out, and bowed my head while saying, "Father in the name of Jesus, I pray for this young man, this warrior. I ask that you would reveal your love; your great plan for his life, and give him a great job. I thank you that you hear me Father, In Jesus name. Amen."

He thanked me, mentioned that he had to be going, and left the room.

One of the men sitting on the adjacent bench from me said, "Man, I can't believe that just happened. I can't believe you just prayed for that guy, *and he let you!*" He indicated that he too was a Christian and commended me for loving that guy and praying for him. We talked for another five minutes or so, until we were interrupted by the young man as he opened the door and came back into the sauna.

He looked at me and said, "Hey, I just want to tell you something. I never have let someone pray for me and I don't really do religious stuff...but when you prayed for me, I mean, when I went back outside, I could *feel* my heart jumping. I just want to thank you."

I told him simply, "That's Jesus..." He left with a smile on his face.

I still see the young man from time to time at the gym and he always smiles at me and gives me a hug, telling me about the things that are going on in his life.

I always try to point him to Jesus' teachings and remind him..."You are a warrior, you were made to be strong."

Strength

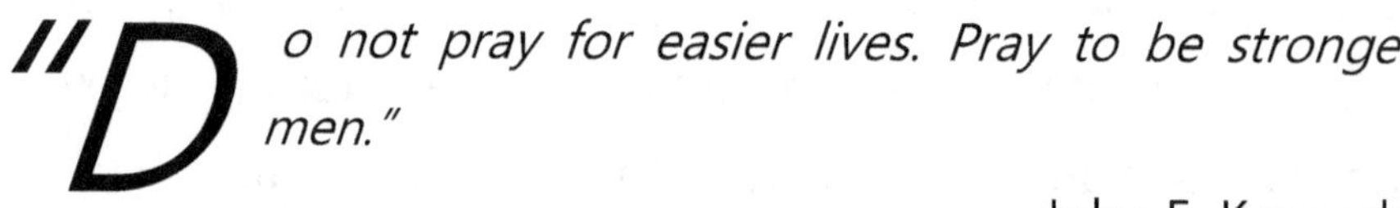

"Do not pray for easier lives. Pray to be stronger men."

– John F. Kennedy

Four Key Points:

I. A Man Must be Strong

II. There are Two Types of Strength

III. Strength is Demonstrated When We Make a Stand Against Wrong

IV. Strength of Spirit is the Mark of A Real Man

Four Key Verses:

I. *If you fail under pressure, your strength is too small.* (Proverbs 24:10)

II. *But you will receive power when the Holy Spirit comes upon you.* (Acts 1:8)

III. *Stand your ground, putting on the belt of truth and the body armor of God's righteousness.* (Ephesians 6:14)

IV. *I am going where everyone on earth must someday go. Take courage and be a man.* (1 Kings 2:2)

Strength Point I:

A Man Must be Strong

I can remember one of my earliest treks to the zoo on an elementary school field trip. I was so excited. Our class would be touring the zoo to see the wild animals up close and personal. I remember seeing the monkeys, and the silver backed gorillas. There were birds of every kind. Zebras, giraffes, the whole spectrum was represented. But there was one beast that I was most anxious to see – the Lion. This majestic brute was the king of the jungle. His roar would shake the ground and could be heard for miles. It would paralyze its victims with the sheer power of its ferocity. I had seen him on television and read about him in books.

The big moment came. I followed the signs that pointed to the area that housed the "King of the Jungle." When I looked up and saw the sign, I was really excited. It said "Lion" and pointed in the direction I should go.

I started running. I rounded the corner to see this Lion. I was not prepared for what I saw. I stopped in my tracks. Like a splash of cold water in the face, my expectations where sadly dampened. There in a pathetic mound of fur was a pathetic excuse of a large cat. He looked half asleep and uninterested in everyone around him. People were shouting and waving their arms to get the Lion to respond. After a few minutes, it became clear to me that this Lion was not like the ones I had seen before. Somehow, the captivity had drained him of his original glory. His eyes no longer looked fierce, piercing, or even alive. He had lost his roar.

Many men are much like that Lion. I see it in their eyes when I talk with them. Captivity of broken relationships, dull and disinteresting or even comfortable lives have robbed them of their roar.

Men were created to be Lions of Masculinity, Strength, and love. You were created to be a dangerous man and you were made to ROAR!

One of the main points of manhood is strength. It is a characteristic that sets us apart from women. Men are physically stronger. We are given this strength to accomplish manly tasks and also to fight and defend our families if necessary. Men are created to be warriors and a weak warrior is a dead warrior.

As a man, it is important to develop strength in many different areas. Strength comes naturally in some men, but others have to work harder to develop strength.

A great example of a man who was not born strong, but became strong is Theodore Roosevelt. Teddy Roosevelt was born a small, weak, sickly child with Asthma so severe that he could not even get out of bed some days. He was not able to play and develop like other children. This left him small, weak, and frail. His father told him when he was a young teen, "Theodore, you have the mind, but you have not the body, and without the help of the body, the mind cannot go as far as it should. You must make your body." Teddy answered, "I will make my body!" Theodore Roosevelt then began a rigorous program of pushing himself to his limits by boxing, wrestling, swimming, hunting, and hiking.

This rigorous self-inflicted routine caused him to become tenacious in every area. He was a voracious reader, a hard worker, and a formidable political opponent. His diligent and courageous work ethic caused him to be promoted through the ranks until he became 26th President of the United States. During his years as President, he would often spend time as a cowboy on cattle drives and big game hunting around the world. The secret service had to stop him from attempting to catch wolves by grabbing them by the bottom jaw as they attacked with a friend in Oklahoma.

Once during a speech, an assassination attempt was made on his life. While standing at a podium delivering a speech, he was shot in the chest by a crazed saloonkeeper. After the man was arrested and Roosevelt realized that the wound did not hit any vital organs, he continued his speech for over an hour, bleeding through his shirt and was then rushed to the hospital.

What physical strength he lacked in his childhood, he more than compensated for by pushing his body to exertion in every area. This made him a strong and formidable man.

Another man born with a similar frail build and inherent weakness was Winston Churchill. He was said to be scrawny and possess the hands of a girl. Because of his weak build, during his teenage life he pushed himself to never back away from a physical challenge. He once jumped from a 30 ft bridge during a game of tag and was knocked unconscious for three days.

This type of commitment to make himself strong helped him to lead the United Kingdom through its darkest and most dangerous hours, the Nazi invasion by Hitler.

God did not create us to be angels. He did not create us to be women. He created us to be men and therefore requires us to be manly, not feminine.

There has been a lot of talk about a man's "feminine side". But if you read the Biblical account of Genesis, you'll see that Man's feminine side was removed when he took Eve from out of Adam.

Fruit Trees produce fruit. Oysters produce pearls. Men produce manhood, and manhood requires strength.

Strength Point II:

There are Two Types of Strength

Another necessary strength for a man to possess is spiritual strength. A man can be strong physically, yet cave at the first sign of adversity because he lacks spiritual strength.

Spiritual strength is what keeps a man pushing forward when his physical strength is failing. Proverbs says,

"The human spirit can endure a sick body, but who can bear a crushed spirit? (Proverbs 18:14)

It is in tough times when we are physically unable to do something to change a situation, that our spiritual strength will cause us to be strong.

A great example of this type of inward strength is found in the US Navy Seals. Driven to exhaustion, physical failure, fatigue, and danger, they are trained to never quit, and never give up, even in the face of insurmountable odds.

Popularized by the movie, "Lone Survivor" the story of Mike Murphy is told describing unswerving courage, commitment, and selfless sacrifice.

Lt. Michael Murphy was a US Navy Seal serving in Afghanistan. His team was sent to Afghanistan to locate a high-level militia leader. During this mission, they were discovered by a large number of Taliban and were engaged in a firefight.

When Lt. Murphy saw that their situation was impossible, and communication had failed, he then climbed to an area that would give them communication signal, but would also mean that he would almost certainly be shot and killed, although he could help his men get reinforcements. Facing certain death, he went for it. He was killed while saving his team. He received the Medal of Honor, posthumously along with the respect and admiration of a grateful country. Here is an excerpt from his official commendation:

THIS DELIBERATE, HEROIC ACT DEPRIVED HIM OF COVER, EXPOSING HIM TO DIRECT ENEMY FIRE. FINALLY ACHIEVING CONTACT WITH HIS HEADQUARTERS, LIEUTENANT MURPHY MAINTAINED HIS EXPOSED POSITION WHILE HE PROVIDED HIS LOCATION AND REQUESTED IMMEDIATE SUPPORT FOR HIS TEAM. IN HIS FINAL ACT OF BRAVERY, HE CONTINUED TO ENGAGE THE ENEMY UNTIL HE WAS MORTALLY WOUNDED, GALLANTLY GIVING HIS LIFE FOR HIS COUNTRY AND FOR THE CAUSE OF FREEDOM. BY HIS SELFLESS LEADERSHIP, COURAGEOUS ACTIONS, AND EXTRAORDINARY DEVOTION TO DUTY, LIEUTENANT MURPHY REFLECTED GREAT CREDIT UPON HIMSELF AND UPHELD THE HIGHEST TRADITIONS OF THE UNITED STATES NAVAL SERVICE."

Lt. Murphy, far right, risked his life in order to send a distress call for his team.

Strength Point III:

Strength is Demonstrated When We Make a Stand Against Wrong

Being from Texas, some of my favorite stories are those of the Texas Rangers. The Rangers were a group of tough, Wild West lawmen that would stand up against seemingly insurmountable odds and enforce the law and commands of their superior officers.

One such story is that of William "Captain Bill" McDonald. The story goes that during the late 1800's there was a large crowd gathering for an illegal boxing match in Dallas. The Governor of Texas had sent the directive that the match be shut down. The Mayor of Dallas was concerned that a riot would ensue when the match was stopped. He sent for the aid of the Texas Rangers. A train soon arrived and the Mayor was expecting to see a large force of rangers dismount the train. What he saw instead was a young Bill McDonald step off the train wearing the silver star of the Texas Rangers carrying only his bag and Winchester rifle. The Mayor quickly asked, "where are the others?" To which the young man replied, "Only one riot, so only one Ranger." This became the motto of the Texas Rangers. McDonald calmed the fears of the Mayor and also stopped the crowd from rioting.

Captain Bill was also quoted as saying "No man in the wrong can stand up against a fellow that's in the right and keeps on a-comin." Those words have evolved into the Ranger creed. (Texas Department of Public Safety)

In the Bible, we are taught the inspiring story of David, who single handedly demonstrated strength by killing Goliath and hacking his head off with his own sword. David's Strength was his abandon, confidence, and faith that God would show up, or David would die trying.

Strength Point IV:

Strength of Spirit is the Mark of A Real Man

"*It is curious that physical courage should be so common in the world and moral courage so rare.*" - Mark Twain

A man can be physically strong and yet without spiritual strength, he will fail. Case in point – Simon, later renamed Peter by Jesus, was the head of a fishing operation. He ran boats, gave orders, and fished the sea daily to make a living. He was a rough outdoorsman. He was introduced to Jesus by his brother Peter and immediately gave up everything to follow Him. He was an impetuous, all-or-nothing kind of guy. He would dare to do things that others would not.

When Jesus came to the disciples walking on the water, Peter was the first one to step out of the boat and *walk on water.* When the high priests guards came and arrested Jesus in the garden, Peter was ready to go. He pulled out his sword and hacked into the side of the guard's head, severing his ear from his skull. He was a quick tempered, passionate, and strong man. He had promised Jesus that "though all forsake him," he would not. But he lacked spiritual strength.

When Jesus was arrested and on his way to mock trial and crucifixion, his disciples, which included Peter, were scattered and in hiding. During this time, a small girl later approached Peter and said, "This man was with him." But Peter denied her claims by saying, "Woman, I don't know him."

When it came time to make a stand, Peter was unable to because he lacked the spiritual strength to make a stand for Jesus. We will be faced with similar days. We will be counted on to stand up for Jesus in our lives at one time or another and whether we stand or fall will be determined by our spiritual strength.

We flash forward into Peter's life and see him standing up before a crowd of over 3,000 people. He is emphatically and unashamedly proclaiming Jesus and displaying huge spiritual strength.

What happened? What is different now that made him so strong? The answer to these questions, along with the secret to our own spiritual strength can be found in Acts, Chapter 2. This is where Peter received his spiritual strength. It is also where we can receive ours today.

"On the day of Pentecost all the believers were meeting together in one place. Suddenly, there was a sound from heaven like the roaring of a mighty windstorm, and it filled the house where they were sitting. Then, what looked like flames or tongues of fire appeared and settled on each of them. And everyone present was filled with the Holy Spirit and began speaking in other languages, as the Holy Spirit gave them this ability." (Acts 2:1-4)

The secret to his spiritual power and ours as men is the Holy Spirit. God's Holy Spirit gives us the power we need to stand for God and have the inner strength that we need to be real men. Jesus told his followers:

"But you will receive power when the Holy Spirit comes upon you. And you will be my witnesses, telling people about me everywhere--in Jerusalem, throughout Judea, in Samaria, and to the ends of the earth." (Acts 1:8)

Teamwork:

Pray together and ask God to fill you with his Holy Spirit power. Pray something similar to this:

"Father, in Jesus Name I ask you to fill me with the Holy Spirit and power just like you did in Peter's life. Your Holy Word promises that if I ask, you will fill me. I believe and I now receive it. I thank you now. In Jesus Name, Amen."

LESSON 7

CORE VALUES

Core Values

One man who stands out among most men in the book of Genesis, is Abram. He was a man of conviction and values that separated him from all the men of his age. His character was such that when offered great riches from a King, he refused them and said *"I will not take so much as a single thread or sandal thong from what belongs to you. Otherwise, you might say, 'I am the one who made Abram rich.'"* (Genesis 14:23)

Abram's character was strong and resolute and distinguished him from even his family. It was enough that God called him *"My friend."*

Throughout the biblical account of Abram, we are told that he built altars to the Lord, representative of his great love and devotion to God. He also lived a nomadic life in tents. It was said that he "built his altars" and he "pitched his tents." One denotes the substance of building solid and the other denotes the temporary and fluid nature of pitching.

As men, we often confuse our focus on personality rather than character. Men spend time building their personality; their charm, demeanor, presentation, looks, talking skills, while pitching their character. As true men of substance, we must focus on building our character and core values, while pitching our personality and charm as secondary values to our own character. Then we will be men like Abraham, whom God chose to be His friend.

"Associate yourself with men of good quality if you esteem your own reputation, for 'tis better to be alone than in bad company." - George Washington

Core Values

Just like the name implies, core values are the values at the very core of who we are. Like a compass, our core values lead us through the decisions we make in life. The core values we have will guide our thoughts. Our thoughts will determine what sort of actions we take. Those actions, in turn will determine our habits. The habits will dictate our lifestyle, and our lifestyle will determine our destiny.

A man's destiny is determined by his core values and habits that he creates.

When we set our core values, we set the course for our life. If we don't define our core values, something else will.

Four Key Points:

I. Core Values Determine our Direction in Life

II. Core Values Define our Legacy

III .Core Values are Demonstrated by our Traditions

IV. Core Values are Shaped by our Associations

Four Key Verses:

I. *Walk with the wise and become wise; associate with fools and get in trouble.* (Proverbs 13:20)

II. *How joyful are those who fear the LORD.* (Psalm 128: 1-4)

III. *As a man thinks in his heart, so is he."* (Proverbs 23: 7)

IV. *Repeat them again and again to your children. Talk about them when you are at home and when you are on the road, when you are going to bed and when you are getting up.* (Deuteronomy 6:7)

Core Values Point I:

Core Values Determine Direction in Life

Every decision we make in life is run through the filter of our core values. If one of the core values you have determined is that "it's OK to do whatever it takes to survive", when the decision comes to lie, cheat, or steal, you will end up in a situation that could bring potential negative consequences to you and all those who follow you.

Bernie Madoff was a New York financier and investment broker. He began and managed the investment firm that handled billions of dollars from influential businessmen and was actually a chairman of the NASDAQ. Over the years, Madoff stole billions of dollars from investors in what is called the largest financial fraud scheme in U.S. History. Bernie Madoff became a billionaire and enjoyed the wealth of the super elite, for a season. Bernie became a suspect in a criminal investigation and was discovered by the authorities. He was later convicted and sentenced to 150 years in prison. Two years after his conviction, one of his sons tragically committed suicide. His second son died of Lymphoma shortly after. Bernie Madoff sits penniless in prison, his family destroyed, and his life decimated. Madoff's core values somewhere allowed him to determine that stealing from others was acceptable as long as he became wealthier. These core values determined a destiny of destruction for him and his entire family, along with the countless people who lost money to his thefts. A sad outcome from a lack of core values.

To be effective, core values are best determined *prior* to times of testing. I always tell the young men I mentor that their "back-seat" theology needs to be determined before they decide to go on a date with a girl. I tell them that if they "wait till they are in the back seat of a car alone with a girl to determine how far they'll go, they've already lost the battle. The best men I know already have a list of non-negotiables that they live by in any given situation. The very best core values are those that are centered around and anchored in the 10 Commandments from Deuteronomy 20 and Exodus 5:

1. You shall have no other gods before Me.

2. You shall not make idols.

3. You shall not take the name of the LORD your God in vain.

4. Remember the Sabbath day, to keep it holy.

5. Honor your father and your mother.

6. You shall not murder.

7. You shall not have sex outside of marriage.

8. You shall not steal.

9. You shall not lie about your neighbor.

10. You shall not lust after other people's things.

These original 10 core values given by God establish a rule for our conduct, that if correctly followed will allow for the healthiest, happiest, and most fulfilling life. Conversely, if we choose to break these, we set in motion a pattern of destruction for our families and ourselves for generations to come.

Core Values Point II:

Core Values Define our Legacy

Core values should not only be the guiding principles in our life, they should be passed from generation to generation. They become the essence of a family. Have you ever spent time with a strong family and noticed that there are distinctives that make the family different? As a man, we are the spiritual architects of our homes.

An interesting story is told by God in the Book of the Prophet Jeremiah concerning core values established and set forth by a family:

This is the message the LORD gave Jeremiah when Jehoiakim son of Josiah was king of Judah: "Go to the settlement where the families of the Recabites live, and invite them to the LORD's Temple. Take them into one of the inner rooms, and offer them some wine."

So I went to see Jaazaniah son of Jeremiah and grandson of Habazziniah and all his brothers and sons— representing all the Recabite families. 4 I took them to the Temple, and we went into the room assigned to the sons of Hanan son of Igdaliah, a man of God. This room was located next to the one used by the Temple officials, directly above the room of Maaseiah son of Shallum, the Temple gatekeeper.

I set cups and jugs of wine before them and invited them to have a drink, but they refused. "No," they said, "we don't drink wine, because our ancestor Jehonadab son of Recab gave us this command: 'You and your descendants must never drink wine. And do not build houses or plant crops or vineyards, but always live in tents. If you follow these commands, you will live long, good lives in the land.' So we have obeyed him in all these things. We have never had a drink of wine to this day, nor have our wives, our sons, or our daughters. We haven't built houses or owned vineyards or farms or planted crops. We have lived in tents and have fully obeyed all the commands of Jehonadab, our ancestor. But when King Nebuchadnezzar of Babylon attacked this country, we were afraid of the Babylonian and Syrian armies. So we decided to move to Jerusalem. That is why we are here."

Then the LORD gave this message to Jeremiah: "This is what the LORD of Heaven's Armies, the God of Israel, says: Go and say to the people in Judah and Jerusalem, 'Come and learn a lesson about how to obey me. The Recabites do not drink wine to this day because their ancestor Jehonadab told them not to. But I have spoken to you again and again, and you refuse to obey me. (Jeremiah 35: 1-14)

We set the tone for our household. And not only our immediate family but also those who are to come, *for generations.*

We set this tone by our actions and our actions are a direct reflection of the core values we have established in our own personal lives. Our children will learn more by what we do than by what we say. Children will not always listen to what we say, but they will almost always emulate who we are. More is caught than is taught. When we demonstrate character, prayer, and devotion in our lives, we pass the baton of values to the next generation.

Core Values Point III:

Core Values are Demonstrated by our Traditions

I went to a men's conference where the speaker, Dr. Tony Evans was teaching about Psalm 128. In this Psalm, a Godly family pattern was being described. It said:

I. How joyful are those who fear the LORD—
   All who follow his ways.

II. You will enjoy the fruit of your labor.
   How joyful and prosperous you will be!

III. Your wife will be like a fruitful grapevine,
   flourishing within your home.
   Your children will be like vigorous young olive
   trees as they sit around your table.

IV. That is the LORD's blessing
   for those who fear him. (Psalm 128:1-4)

As he was describing our children flourishing around our table like olive trees, it occurred to me that I didn't even own a table! Any meals that were eaten in my house were generally in the living room, in front of the television. I was immediately convicted and decided to go and buy my family a table to have meals together and provide an atmosphere where I could pour into them and hear their struggles. We would also, from time to time, hold family meetings at that table and discuss everything from family crisis and problems, to planning family vacations together.

The results were notable. Lots of great time spent together. I will never regret that decision to buy the table. A family tradition of shared meals was born that day.

Another notable tradition that we have placed in our home is the family devotion.

Family Devotion

One evening while attending a church service, the guest speaker asked the audience a question, "How many of you have a regularly scheduled weekly time with your family where you study God's word, worship together, and pray for one another as a family. Out of a crowd of 500, only 3 or so raised their hands. I was not able to raise my hand. I knew the value of a family devotional time. I had even made attempts in the past to get us together and do this. Sure, we read the Bible at times, prayed at times, but I had never been intentional about setting a *set* night of the week for us, as a family, to grow together in the Lord.

I was convicted *again.*

That night, I decided that I would "take the bull by the horns." I discussed with my wife that, from this point forward, every Monday night should be our set family night devotional. She agreed.

The first Monday rolled around and the opportunities to do something else appeared from every direction. But we said "no" to those things and "yes" to our family. We first had dinner together as a family-at our table. Then after dinner, we moved into the living room. My son brought out the guitar and led us in two songs. The girls sang and it sounded like angels in our house. After the worship time, we all took our Bibles and I instructed first my oldest daughter, then my middle son, and then my youngest daughter to read a different chapter from the Bible. I didn't put a lot of thought into a theme or where to read, just reading any part was good, and sometimes they seemed to follow a common thread, imagine that.

When we finished the worship and Bible reading, it came time to pray. I began the prayer by praying out loud for my wife. I prayed for her upcoming week and anything else that came to mind. I thanked God for giving me such a Godly, wonderful wife. Then I prayed for each of my children individually, asking God to bless and protect them this upcoming week, along with praying for anything else that came to mind that they might need. Then, it was my wife's turn to pray. She prayed for me, then anything else that came to mind. Then each of my children prayed, starting from the oldest, and working their way down, for whatever was on their heart. By the time we finished praying, we felt closer to God and closer as a family. Then we ate dessert together. This has helped us stay connected and growing as a family. We even started inviting other families over to teach them how to have a family devotional.

Core Values Point IV:

Core Values are Determined by Your Associations

The Vagabonds: Ford, Edison, Harding & Firestone

One of my mentors once told me, "You are changed most by two things in life – the books you read, and the friends you keep. Our friends and our futures are inextricably linked. More than we realize, we are shaped and formed by the company we keep.

What do Thomas Edison, Henry Ford, Harvey Firestone, and Harding have in common? Besides the fact that they were industrial pioneers, entrepreneurs, multi-millionaires and billionaires?

They were friends who regularly spent time with one another thinking, dreaming, debating, and discussing ideas. In his book, Think and Grow Rich, Napoleon Hill introduces the concept of the Mastermind Alliance or Group. The concept states that when great minds come together and think and dream, their collective thoughts take on an exponential power beyond their individual thoughts. The big idea is that when we associate with people who are intelligent and moving forward, we encourage each other to go farther and do more than we would otherwise.

The company we keep also shapes our manhood. I encourage you to spend time with men of substance. Someone once challenged the way I think about my associations by telling me that, "you are the sum total of your five closest friends."

If you hang around five confident people,

you will be the sixth.

If you hang around five intelligent people,

you will be the sixth.

If you hang around five millionaires,

you will be the sixth.

If you hang around five idiots,

you will be the sixth.

Walk with the wise and become wise; associate with fools and get in trouble. (Proverbs 13:20)

The Family Crest

Many great families throughout history have developed a "Family Coat of Arms" or "Family Crest" to represent the values and characteristics of their family. Some of these have been passed down for hundreds of years. Every royal family has their own crest. Developing a family crest is a productive and influential activity to help you, as a family, to remember what is most important to you.

Here is the Rorie Family Crest developed during our devotional time together as a family.

Lion = Courage & Leadership

Heart = Compassion & Love

Sword = Chivalry & Honor

Dove = Holy Spirit & Ministry

Mission 1:

With input from your entire family, develop a family crest or Coat of Arms that symbolizes your four main core values as a family. The crest consists of four symbols that best represent the things your family values most. Although any symbol that you choose is great, here are some examples of symbols that might be used to represent your family's values:

Gauntlet = Strength

Rose = Love

Lion = Courage

Bear = Faithfulness

Bee = Industry or Diligence

Eagle = Leadership

Owl = Wisdom

Cross = Ministry

Heart = Compassion

Flower = Beauty

Harp = Worship

Sword = Chivalry & Honor

You might chose to have the crest professionally designed and displayed in your home and passed to future generations. Fiverr.com is a great place to have graphics developed for as little as $5.00.

Mission 2:

Dad – With input from Mom for scheduling, establish a time to put a set night in place for family devotional using a similar pattern as that mentioned in this chapter. Be sure to include reading the word together, worship, and prayer.

Note: Practice makes perfect. You might feel uncomfortable praying in front of your family, but press through and you will become the spiritual leader your family needs.

Mission 3:

Team - Identify or plan 4 family traditions that should be passed to future generations.

____

____

____

____

____

____

____

LESSON 8

CODE OF

HONOR

Code of Honor

Four Key Points:

I. A Code of Honor should be established by every man to be used in crisis and temptation and as a general rule of conduct.

II. Every warrior class in History has developed and passed a "Code of Honor" to its warriors.

III. Every Man Should Have or Develop a List of "Non-Negotiables."

IV. The Stronger the Code of Honor, the Stronger the Man. The Stronger the Man, the stronger his future will be.

Four Key Scriptures:

I. *Study this Book of Instruction continually. Meditate on it day and night, so you will be sure to obey everything written in it. Only then will you prosper and succeed in all you do.* (Joshua 1:8)

II. *Then God gave the people all these instructions* (Exodus 20:1)

III. *"Anyone who listens to my teaching and follows it is wise, like a person who builds a house on solid rock. 25 Though the rain comes in torrents and the floodwaters rise and the winds beat against that house, it won't collapse because it is built on bedrock. 26 But anyone who hears my teaching and doesn't obey it is foolish, like a person who builds a house on sand. 27 When the rains and floods come and the winds beat against that house, it will collapse with a mighty crash."* (Matthew 7: 24-27)

IV. *Seek the Kingdom of God above all else, and live righteously, and he will give you everything you need.* (Matthew 6:33)

Code of Honor Point I:

A Code of Honor Should be Established by Every Man

We all live by a code of honor. This code emanates from our hearts, from what we feel is right or wrong. Often, we adopt codes of honor from others. It is important that we have guidelines and a code of honor to live by. If we don't establish our own code, we will end up living by someone else's code. When we live according to another man's code, we will share in his consequences as well, whether good or bad. The Lord put forth his code of honor for man to live by that would help him to be successful. The Lord told Joshua:

Study this book of instruction continually. Meditate on it day and night so you will be sure to obey everything written in it. Only then will you prosper and succeed in all you do. (Joshua 1:8)

Code of Honor Point II:

Every Warrior Class in History has Developed a Code of Honor

Throughout history, almost every civilization, organization and warrior class have developed a Code of Honor to outline the values that make them different from others and guide their conduct to achieve the goals that they deem valuable. These society's warriors have developed a Code of Honor which that group seeks to live out to achieve a heroic and brave class of men. This Code has distinguished the group of men from the common or baser class of males. In this chapter, we will examine different Codes of Honor from historic groups and then develop our own code of honor.

Some examples of the Codes of outstanding men are:

The Code of Chivalry

The code of chivalry was a code held to by Medieval Knights. It ruled their conduct and they took vows to uphold this sacred code. It distinguished them from the barbarians of their time. It was also referred to as "The Code of the Knight."

CODE OF THE KNIGHT

I. Thou shalt believe all that the Word of God teaches, and shalt observe all its directions.

II. Thou shalt defend all that is good, all that is right.

III. Thou shalt respect all weaknesses, and shalt constitute thyself the defender of them.

IV. Thou shalt love the country in which thou wast born.

V. Thou shalt not recoil before thine enemy.

VI. Thou shalt make war against tyranny and injustice without cessation, and without mercy.

VII. Thou shalt perform scrupulously thy duties to God.

The Bushido Code

The Bushido code was utilized by the Samurai class warriors of Japan. The code had seven virtues that were expected to be embraced and exhibited by the Samurai. They adhered very closely to this code and it became so ingrained in them that they would often choose to die than to break their sacred code of honor. They went overboard in their code because they placed human life at a lower value than honor.

Some of the elements of the code were:

Righteousness	Bravery
Giving	Respect
Honesty	Honor
Fidelity	

The Code of the West

The Code of the West, also known as the "Cowboy Code" was a set of unwritten rules that cowboys lived for during the days of westward expansion in the United States. They were principles like:

Never shoot a man in the back.

Always protect women and children.

Live with courage.

Take pride in your work.

Always finish what you start.

When you make a promise, keep it.

Always show loyalty to the brand.

Talk less and say more.

French Foreign Legion

- The mission is sacred; you carry it out until the end.

- If necessary in the field, carry out the mission at the risk of your life.

Our Creed

One of the creeds of the Men of Honor groups is also a creed that my son memorized as his personal creed. It is called "The Fellowship of The Unashamed" it can be found in the book by Dr. Edwin Louis Cole entitled "Strong Men in Tough Times."

The Fellowship of the Unashamed

I am part of the "Fellowship of the Unashamed." The die has been cast. The decision has been made. I have stepped over the line. I won't look back, let up, slow down, back away or be still.

My past has been redeemed, my present makes sense, and my future is secure. I'm finished and done with low living, sight walking, small planning, smooth knees, colorless dreams, tamed visions, mundane talking, cheap giving, and dwarfed goals.

I no longer need preeminence, position, promotions, plaudits, or popularity. I don't have to be right, first, tops, recognized, praised, regarded or rewarded.

I now live by faith, lean on His presence, love with patience, live by prayer and labor with power. My face is set, my gait is fast, my goal is heaven, my road is narrow, my way is rough, my companions are few, my Guide is reliable, and my mission is clear.

I cannot be bought, compromised, detoured, lured away, turned back, deluded, or delayed. I will not flinch in the face of sacrifice, hesitate in the presence of adversity, negotiate at the table of the enemy, ponder at the pool of popularity, or meander in the maze of mediocrity.

I won't give up, shut up, let up or slow up until I have stayed up, stored up, prayed up, paid up and spoken up for the cause of Christ.

I am a disciple of Jesus. I must go 'til He comes, give 'til I drop, preach 'til all know and work 'til He stops me. And when He comes for His own, He will have no problem recognizing me. My banner is clear.

I am part of the "Fellowship of the Unashamed."

Code of Honor Point III:

Every Man Should Have or Develop a List of "Non-Negotiables"

Davy Crockett was a frontiersman and Indian fighter from Tennessee. His reputation as a man of conviction and strength made him famous all over the nation. He was a man of strong ideals and had grit about him that caused others to follow him.

Davy Crockett, though he had no formal schooling, served in the Tennessee legislature during the 1800's. He was credited with killing 105 bears in one year.

His most notable action was his part in the defense of Texas freedom against General Santa Anna and also his epic fight and death during the battle of the Alamo on March 6, 1836.

One memorable quote from Crockett- though there are a few- is:

"First make sure you're right, then go ahead."

Crockett's Code of Honor caused him to make strong stands in defense of freedom and to live a life that inspired others.

Our Code of Honor will help us to make tough decisions and guide our actions to be notable, heroic, and perhaps historical.

Benjamin Franklin was an inventor, statesman, and one of the founding fathers of America. He was attributed as saying, "If you fail to plan, you plan to fail." This saying encapsulates the essence of developing a default for decision-making and the code by which we choose to live our lives.

Franklin developed his set of core values and non-negotiables early in life. When he was twenty, while working as a printer, he published these non-negotiables or core values under the title, "The 13 Virtues." Franklin wrote,

"I propos'd to myself, for the sake of clearness, to use rather more names, with fewer ideas annex'd to each, than a few names with more ideas; and I included under thirteen names of virtues all that at that time occurr'd to me as necessary or desirable, and annexed to each a short precept, which fully express'd the extent I gave to its meaning."

Benjamin Franklin

- Temperance. Eat not to dullness; drink not to elevation.

- Silence. Speak not but what may benefit others or yourself; avoid trifling conversation.

- Order. Let all your things have their places; let each part of your business have its time.

- Resolution. Resolve to perform what you ought; perform without fail what you resolve.

- Frugality. Make no expense but to do good to others or yourself; i.e., waste nothing.

- Industry. Lose no time; be always employed in something useful; cut off all unnecessary actions.

- Sincerity. Use no hurtful deceit; think innocently and justly, and, if you speak, speak accordingly.

- Justice. Wrong none by doing injuries, or omitting the benefits that are your duty.

- Moderation. Avoid extremes; forbear resenting injuries so much as you think they deserve.

- Cleanliness. Tolerate no uncleanliness in body, clothes, or habitation.

- Tranquillity. Be not disturbed at trifles, or at accidents common or unavoidable.

- Chastity. Maintain sexual integrity at all times.

- Humility. Imitate Jesus and Socrates.

Franklin believed that if a person lived by these virtues and sought to develop these values into ones life, that person would be a person of character. Obviously he found that these virtues certainly helped him to be successful as he became the first Postmaster General, invented and held many patents for new inventions, founded two colleges, started the first insurance company, founded the first hospital, the first circulating library, first U.S. police and fire department, invented a musical instrument, owned and operated several businesses, was the first person to map the gulf stream, enabling faster sea travel, was the Ambassador to England and was one of the chief architects of the U.S. Constitution.

Code of Honor Point IV:

The Stronger the Code of Honor, the Stronger the Man. The Stronger the Man, the Stronger his Future will be.

The foundation of our Code will determine the strength of our lives. If our foundation is weak, then everything built upon it will be suspect. But if we build on a strong and proven foundation, we will experience strength of life and stability of accomplishments. Jesus told a story about this process in the Gospel of Matthew by illustrating two builders.

"Anyone who listens to my teaching and follows it is wise, like a person who builds a house on solid rock. Though the rain comes in torrents and the floodwaters rise and the winds beat against that house, it won't collapse because it is built on bedrock. But anyone who hears my teaching and doesn't obey it is foolish, like a person who builds a house on sand. 27 When the rains and floods come and the winds beat against that house, it will collapse with a mighty crash." (Matthew 7: 24-27)

When we base our non-negotiables and Code of Honor on the Word of God, we will ensure success for our lives and those that come after us.

Seek the Kingdom of God above all else, and live righteously, and he will give you everything you need. (Matthew 6:33)

Mission:

Dad: Share a few of your "non-negotiables" with your son. These should be brief statements of your personal beliefs that he can take as his own creed.

____

____

____

____

____

____

____

Team – Father & Son – Using some of the examples in this chapter, develop your own personal Code of Honor that will help you both and can also be passed down to future generations.

____

____

____

____

____

____

LESSON 9

THE HEART OF A MAN

The Heart of a Man

Joe was a young good-looking 16-year-old from a rough past of broken family and broken dreams. His father, an army veteran had come back from his time in the service with severe depression and began drinking heavily. As is the case with heavy drinking, the depression only deepened until Joe's father one day took his own life.

Joe told me that he remembered hearing the shot that ended his father's life. He then spent time living with his mom and eventually, her boyfriend who was a hard and discouraging influence in Joe's life. Joe looked for satisfaction and release through drugs and sex, but there were no answers to be found there.

Joe wandered into one of our Men of Honor groups in Rowlett, Texas after a friend invited him to the after school group for guys his age. He sat in the back and after hearing the message that Jesus could give anyone a new heart, he committed his life to Christ. Joe continued to come to the meetings and learned more about the new life available in Christ. He took in every teaching eagerly. He was very shy and quiet and spent most of his time quietly watching the lesson from the back row. One day during class, I asked Joe if he would share his story with the rest of the group.

I was not ready for what happened. Joe stepped up to the front and this quiet, shy, reserved young man began sharing God's word passionately and eloquently to the rest of the group with the fiery zeal of a seasoned evangelist.

I didn't even recognize him. He completely transformed before our eyes. I realized then and remarked to the co-leader helping me, "This is not flesh and blood we are watching. It is what happens when God's Spirit comes into a willing vessel. HE takes over and makes men into something new." Joe stayed in touch with me over the next few weeks, and would call me when something big happened. One day he called me and said, "There were about twenty people getting high out behind the school one day and I walked up in the middle of them and began to share verses from the Bible with them and telling them that God loves them. Most of them ran off immediately, but two stayed and let me pray with them to receive Christ. A week or so later he called me saying, "Mr. Rorie, I just baptized two kids in my bathtub. On one of them, their feet didn't go all the way under, does that count?" "Yes Joe, it counts," I quickly answered. Joe radically changed because his heart radically changed. A new heart makes a new man.

The Heart of A Man

"Because God has made us for Himself, our hearts are restless until they rest in Him." —Augustine

Four Key Points:

I. It All Starts in the Heart

II. Guarding your Heart

III. Your Heart Needs to Forgive & Be Forgiven

IV. A New Heart

Four Key Verses:

I. *And then he (Jesus) added, "It is what comes from inside that defiles you."* (Mark 7:20-23)

II. *"Guard your heart above all else, for it determines the course of your life."* (Proverbs 4:23)

III. *If you forgive the sins of any, they are forgiven them; if you retain the sins of any, they are retained."* (John 20:23-25 NKJV)

IV. And I will give you a new heart, and I will put a new spirit in you. I will take out your stony, stubborn heart and give you a tender, responsive heart. 27 And I will put my Spirit in you so that you will follow my decrees and be careful to obey my regulations. (Ezekiel 36: 26,27)

It All Starts in The Heart

As men, we like to fix things. We don't like to talk about it, think about, and share about it, we like to get our hands on it and fix it. We have an innate desire to fix things.

Here's where the problem lies; when we try to fix it, we often try in the wrong ways.

When we feel dissatisfied, we try to fix our surroundings, we try to read more books, change the way we act, change the way we speak, and sometimes, change our location. We try new jobs, new homes, new cars, and sometimes-new spouses.

The truth has always been the same; it all begins and ends with our hearts. All problems begin in the heart and end in the heart. Jesus said:

And then he (Jesus) added, "It is what comes from inside that defiles you. For from within, out of a person's heart, come evil thoughts, sexual immorality, theft, murder, adultery, greed, wickedness, deceit, lustful desires, envy, slander, pride, and foolishness. All these vile things come from within; they are what defile you." (Mark 7:20-23)

The origins of all issues in our lives are issues of the heart. And if we want to change those things, we must first change our hearts.

Our heart is a muscle in the center of our chest roughly the size of the fist. It beats, on average 70 beats per minute. That's 4200 beats in an hour, 100,000 beats in a day, 36.5 million beats per year, 2.6 billion times in the average life span. When our heart is sick or damaged, the rest of the body will be sick as well. When that heart stops, we step into eternity.

We've all been to a funeral and seen a loved one or friend's body lying in a casket. We also know that what we see is not the real "them," it's just the shell that is left behind. The part of them that goes into eternity is the heart, or spirit that we are discussing now. It's the real person, the real essence of who we are as a man. It is an eternal heart.

This is the heart that the Bible talks so much about. It's what defines you and makes you a man. This is why it is the most important place to focus our attention.

King Solomon, billed as the wisest and richest man that ever lived, said it like this,

"Guard your heart above all else, for it determines the course of your life." (Proverbs 4:23)

A friend once shared this story with me about David Livingstone, the great missionary explorer of the late 1800's:

From his age of earliest remembrance, David Livingston would sit upon his father's knee and hear stories about Africa, the Dark Continent. From his knee, he could almost smell the smoke of campfires rising above the grass rooftops of a thousand villages and envision the dense and uncharted jungles. He could taste the spray of cascading waterfalls over massive heights and he knew that one day he would take the good news of Jesus Christ to Africa. It became his passion and his destiny.

The day would finally come. Twenty years later, now married, David Livingstone embarked on his missionary journey of exploration. He immediately began charting and evangelizing, village-by-village throughout the hostile country. Through great personal sacrifice and imminent danger, the gospel began to illuminate the darkest regions as this fiery evangelist pursued those lost and blinded by centuries of demonic oppression.

Through villages and jungles, he relentlessly traveled proclaiming salvation through the Name of Jesus. Often caught between tribal wars and skirmishes, he narrowly avoided harm. In one such flight, while running for his life in the dead of night, his eye was lost as he ran into a protruding tree branch in the darkness. But even without the benefit of two eyes, his spiritual vision saw a nation that needed the message of freedom in Christ. David endured great hardship. Natives and wild animals often attacked him. During one such attack, a wild lion mauled his shoulder.

The years of exposure to the sun had so darkened his now leathery skin and the jungle had so marred his countenance that when he returned to England for a visit, many did not recognize him, save for his voice as he spoke.

After visiting England, he returned to Africa for many subsequent expeditions with greater focus and greater determination to preach the Gospel. As time continued, David himself contracted a deadly disease. David cried out to the Lord and said. "I will not leave again. If you want me to live, send medicine."

Some weeks later an Englishman appeared in Africa from England to interview the man so revered as the missionary explorer of Africa. He began to tell Mr. Livingston that he was a swaggering atheist and there was no need in trying to convert him and, for some reason, he was supposed to bring him medicine. With the medicine he needed, David continued from village to village preaching and seeing many delivered from the bondage of sin to which all men without Christ are subject.

His condition grew graver as the years passed by. His body was now failing, yet his spirit and relentless desire continued to press on. Eventually he would have to be carried on a litter from village to village where he would prop himself up and preach to the conversion of his hearers. Exhausted yet undaunted, David Livingston was confronted by one of his servants by his bedside. "You must rest Mr. Livingston, you must sleep!" "No." David Livingston replied, "I must pray for Africa. Please prop me up by my bed to pray."

Hours later, the servant returned to check on his leader. To his amazement, David Livingston had died on his knees, praying for the country that he had given his entire life and strength to evangelize.

The tribal leaders gathered from all areas of the continent to honor this great general of God. They ceremonially wrapped and decorated his body and began a relay to hand carry his body, on a litter, to the coast where an awaiting vessel would carry him back to his homeland for burial.

As the procession reached the shore, those Englishmen waiting to carry his body home were shocked as one of the tribal leaders took out a great knife and cut into the chest of David Livingston. "What are these savages doing?" cried the Englishmen. The Chiefs replied as they cut out something from his chest, "His body may belong to England, but his heart belongs to AFRICA!"

When we die, where will they bury our hearts, spiritually speaking?

Every part of who you are begins and ends in your heart. You can change many things about your life. Where you live, how you look, who your friends are, but until you change your heart, you make no lasting change. If you want to change your life, change your heart. Because our hearts are the most important part of us, we have to focus on our hearts before anything else. The heart is also the most important part of us because it is intended to be the dwelling place of God.

Guard Your Heart

In the last point we brought out one verse that commands us to guard our hearts. It is:

"Guard your heart above all else, for it determines the course of your life." (Proverbs 4:23)

Like a soldier guarding his position from hostile enemy forces, it is important that we guard our core, our heart.

Forces that would seek to destroy us are always trying to besiege our hearts. The walls are impenetrable, but the gates are weak. Therefore, we have to guard the gates of our hearts to ensure our castle is strong and unconquerable.

The Eye Gate

Lust is a formidable enemy to our hearts. It can infect and consume our hearts if we are not careful. We were made as very visual creatures. Jesus told us that our eyes are the gates to the soul. If we want to guard our souls, we must guard our eyes.

Unfortunately, this is the weakest gate of our castle. Fortunately, we have control of the gate. The enemies of lust and addiction can sneak in if we don't immediately shut this gate during time of attack. One of the practical ways to close the eye gate is to purpose in your heart not to look at things you know will allow the wrong things in.

Refuse to stay on a TV channel that has improper images. Refuse to look at pornography on your computer, phone, or anywhere. But what can you do about those things that bombard the eye gate without your consent? Here's what we recommend:

The Two-Look Rule:

It is impossible not to see beautiful girls. The first time they cross your vision, there is nothing you can do about it. Immediately your mind will say, Wow! Did you see that?

But the trouble begins when your mind says, "Look back at her again!" Here is where you have the power of choice. You can look again and start the lust engine or you can make a promise, like Job did, and not look a second time. It's when you dwell on an image that it gets access to your heart. Stop lust before it gets into your heart. Just look the other way.

Guard your eyes, guard your heart.

The eyes are the gate entrance to your heart. You can control what gets into your heart by what you allow your eyes to see.

The Ear Gate

Discouragement and depression can come in like a flood if we allow the voices to get in through our ear gates. Music, like computer programming can get a foothold into our thought life. We must not allow negative voices to get in our ears. We guard this by watching over and stopping bad influences coming in through the music we listen to and the words of people that we allow to speak into our lives.

It's OK to say, "My ears are not trash cans in which you may put your trash."

Allow the words of encouragement and compliments to enter your heart, bring in the things that will strengthen your heart, reject the things that try to tear your heart down. Do this and be strong.

Your Heart Needs to Forgive, and be Forgiven

One of the surest ways to poison your heart and stunt your spiritual growth as a man is to refuse to forgive someone.

Like a poison, unforgiveness will stop you dead in your tracks and keep you in an arrested state. Someone once said that refusing to forgive is like drinking poison and waiting for the other person to die. Unforgiveness can also keep you out of heaven. It's just that serious.

When you refuse to forgive someone of a sin, you attach the sin to your heart and it stays there until you forgive. Many men are carrying a great load of sin because of unforgiveness. Jesus said it like this,

If you forgive the sins of any, they are forgiven them; if you retain the sins of any, they are retained." (John 20:23-25 NKJV)

Forgiveness releases sin out of our lives, unforgiveness retains or binds sin to us.

The way that a sin is passed from one generation to the next is through unforgiven sin. The best way and the only way to avoid passing sin from fathers to sons is to forgive and release sin out of the heart.

Forgiveness doesn't mean that you think what they did is O.K. It simple means that you choose to release it out of your life. It means that you want to obey God and have a strong heart more than you want to get revenge. After all, God is willing to forgive us for *anything* and *everything*. Shouldn't we be at least willing to forgive someone for *something*?

Next, we need to *be* forgiven

There is only one way that sin can come out of your life. It can only come out of your mouth, as you confess your sin to God and ask for His forgiveness. Fortunately, God wants to forgive us more that we want to be forgiven. He made a way by sending his Son to become sin and be punished for our sin, so that we don't have to be punished.

Romans 3:23 tells us that:

"All have sinned and come short of the Glory of God"

Romans 6:23 tells us that:

"The wages of sin is death, but the gift of God is eternal life through Christ Jesus."

And to prove how "gung-ho" God is about forgiving you, He took the first step:

"But God demonstrated His love for us, in that while we were yet sinners, Christ died for us." (Romans 5:8)

Also, it does not matter who you are or what you've done. He promised that if we confess our sins, He would forgive them by saying:

"But if we confess our sins to him, he is faithful and just to forgive us our sins and to cleanse us from all wickedness." (1 John 1:9)

It also doesn't matter who you are or what you've done.

God's gift of a new heart is a gift waiting to be accepted. The only way a man can receive a new heart is by allowing God to take away his old heart and give him a new one. He (The LORD) promises:

And I will give you a new heart, and I will put a new spirit in you. I will take out your stony, stubborn heart and give you a tender, responsive heart. 27 And I will put my Spirit in you so that you will follow my decrees and be careful to obey my regulations. (Ezekiel 36: 26,27)

You can accept the free gift by stopping right now and asking God to give you a new heart.

He sent His son Jesus to pay for our sins and wash us clean again.

"Therefore if any man be in Christ, he is a new creature: old things are passed away; behold, all things are become new." (2 Corinthians 5:17)

Mission:

Read through the following prayer together. When you are ready, and this prayer reflects what you feel in your heart, say the prayer aloud together, inviting Jesus into your hearts.

"Dear God,

I realize that I need you in my life, please forgive me for trying to live without you. I know that I have messed up and sinned against you. Please forgive me.

I believe that Jesus died on the cross, shedding His blood for my sins. Please make me clean and new.

I believe Jesus rose again from the dead and I ask Jesus to come and live in my heart, and give me new life.

I give you my life and surrender my heart to you.
Thank you for hearing my prayer, Thank you that I am now saved in Jesus' name."

If you prayed that prayer, you have been forgiven. The Bible says that you are a new person, with a new heart.

Now, it is time for you to allow God to change your life and help you overcome the things that used to hold you back.

Activity for Dads:

Make a list of every person that you have unforgiveness toward. Pray and ask God to reveal them to you, so that you can be sure. Next, spend some time in prayer asking God to help you release their sins out of your life. One by one, say their name and say, "I choose to forgive________" and say their name. Then ask God to forgive you of holding unforgiveness in your heart toward that person. God will hear and will release you. (You don't have to share the list with anyone.)

____

____

____

____

____

____

____

____

____

____

Activity for Sons:

Make a list of every person that you have unforgiveness toward. Pray and ask God to reveal them to you, so that you can be sure. Next, spend some time in prayer asking God to help you release their sins out of your life. One by one, say their name and say, "I choose to forgive______" and say their name. Then ask God to forgive you of holding unforgiveness in your heart toward that person. God will hear and will release you.
(You don't have to share the list with anyone.)

____

____

____

____

____

____

Additional Team Mission:

The next step after salvation is Baptism. Baptism is an outward display of what has just happened inside you. Baptism represents Jesus' death, burial, and resurrection.

When you go under the water you are in fact saying, "The old person that I used to be is dying and when I come out of the water, I am coming out a new man with all my sins washed away."

Plan a time with your Pastor that you can be baptized together. Dad, ask the Pastor if he will baptize you and then allow you to baptize your son.

Send invitations to family and friends telling them about this powerful time when you will both publicly proclaim Jesus as Lord. It's going to be awesome!

LESSON 10

SEXUAL

INTEGRITY

Sexual Integrity

Jay was an outstanding young man. Everyone liked him and he was a natural leader. He was a regular guy who liked the same things everyone else his age liked; guitars, cars, girls, music, girls, art, and girls. One year Jay attended a conference with a few other guys that went to his school. There, Jay was challenged to think differently about how he felt toward God and specifically about the place that God took in his life. In the overall scale of priority in his life, Jay realized that God did not have a very high ranking. Jay made a decision that night that would forever change his life. He decided to put God first in every area of his life. One area that would be deeply impacted by this decision was the area of girls and dating. Jay decided that he was going to put God first and even decided to do something drastic! Jay made a vow or promise to God to give the first part of his teen years to God as a sacrifice; He vowed to date no one but God for a year. He vowed not to date girls for one year! For some guys this would be easy, but Jay had girls calling him all the time.

When you give God the first of anything, he will bless the rest and make it greater than it would have been otherwise.

After Jay's year was up God had blessed his life in an unbelievable way; his musical talents were multiplying and growing at an amazing rate. He was writing and recording songs, performing in many new venues and would soon become a talented and rising star. Jay's life would never be the same because he decided to put God first.

Sexual Integrity

"My strength is as the strength of ten, because my heart is pure." – Alfred Lord Tennyson

Four Key Points:

I. Sexual Integrity is A Battle to Be Won

II. Your Battle Must Have Strategy

III. What we Feed Grows

IV. Real Men Honor Women

Four Key Verses:

I. *"For the weapons of our warfare are not fleshly, but mighty through God to the pulling down of strongholds, pulling down imaginations and every high thing that exalts itself against the knowledge of God, and bringing into captivity every thought into the obedience of Christ,"* (2 Corinthians 10: 4-5 MKJV)

II. *"Likewise, husbands, live together according to knowledge, giving honor to the wife as to the weaker vessel, the female, as truly being co-heirs together of the grace of life, not cutting off your prayers."* (1 Peter 3:7 MKJV)

III. *"But I say to you that whoever looks on a woman to lust after her has already committed adultery with her in his heart."* (Matthew 5:28 MKJV)

IV. *"For if, through the transgression of the one individual, Death made use of the one individual to seize the sovereignty, all the more shall those who receive God's overflowing grace and gift of righteousness reign as kings in Life through the one individual, Jesus Christ."* (Romans 5:17 WNT)

Sexual Integrity

Those who learn about sex from pornography or friends won't know the first ting about it. Namely, why God created it. After all, God created sex and it was Him who declared that it was good.

God gave man incredible creative power. In fact, we are told that God made man to "be like God." (Genesis) He gave man a most precious and powerful gift; He gave him the power to create. He gave him power to reproduce and be like God with the power to create life.

It's no wonder that Satan attacks men most in this area, because of its great power. He knows that if he can pervert God's plan, he can steal the power.

Sexual Integrity is A Battle to Be Won

To keep oneself pure from sex before marriage is to be a virgin. Virginity is the strength and glory of a young man's manhood.

Your virginity is a powerful gift; something that you can give only one time in one lifetime, to one person, and then it's gone. It is a once-in-a-lifetime opportunity.

Dan would often have friends who would ridicule him and make fun of him for being a virgin. But it never bothered him, because in his heart he knew that he was special. He could go out and have sex and be like them, but they could never again be like him. He kept the glory of his manhood, he kept his virginity. He was saving it for his wife, on their wedding day. He would marry the most beautiful woman in all the world (to him) and give her the most valuable gift that he could give her, his virginity. He would remain a champion for her.

Your Battle Must Have Strategy

How do we fight? We fight this battle in our hearts and in our minds. One of the greatest ways to fight is to fight with our eyes open.

Satan wants to destroy you and cause you to fail. He does this by bombarding your eyes and mind with impure sexual images.

God has given us powerful tools to tear down the fantasies and imagination tactics that the enemy uses to get our minds cluttered with images and thoughts that weaken us. They are Holy Spirit powered cleansing agents that clean our minds and destroy those wicked images.

> *"For the weapons of our warfare are not fleshly, but mighty through God to the pulling down of strongholds, pulling down imaginations and every high thing that exalts itself against the knowledge of God, and bringing into captivity every thought into the obedience of Christ;" (2 Corinthians 10: 4-5 MKJV)*

Not every thought you think is yours. Have you ever had a crazy thought enter your mind that was so sick and twisted that you couldn't believe that you thought it? Often times those thoughts are not your own, but the enemy plants those thoughts in your mind. You have to battle those thoughts. One guy told me, "I have even shook my head and hit my head to stop myself from thinking bad thoughts."

Fight the Enemy Where He Attacks

Our first weapon that we use to battle our thoughts is The Word of God – The Bible. It is called the "Sword of the Spirit." To effectively use this sword, we must take it where the battle is -into our thought lives. We must spend time every day thinking about scriptures and allowing them to clean our minds.

Don't Wake Love Before It's Time

Often times when my kids were little, I would have events that would bring me home late at night. When I came home, they were already in bed fast asleep. Because I opened a door too loud or turned on a light too close to their room, they would sometimes wake up and come to see me, thinking it was time to wake up. I would simply pick them up, take them back to their beds and tell them "It's not time to get up, go back to sleep." And off to sleep they would go.

The same is true for feelings of sexual desire. If they have been awakened too early, they need to be put back to sleep, until the time is right.

What We Feed, Grows

Things grow when they are fed, and starve when they are not. Sexual desire is something that can be starved or fed. Through images that are viewed or thoughts that are entertained, we feed sexual desire. We have the power to say "no" to those things and weaken the desire. A dog can beat a lion, if you starve the lion long enough.

An Indian chief once told his son, "I have two dogs fighting inside of me, one very dark and evil, one very strong and good." The son asked him, "Which one wins?" The chief replied, "The one I feed the most."

We have two natures inside of us, the flesh and the spirit. If we feed and follow our flesh, it will always lead us to ruin. But if we feed and follow our spirit we will win in life.

How do we feed our flesh? Bad movies, bad Internet, bad music, bad thoughts, always looking for comfort, and being lazy.

How do we feed our spirit? Reading the Bible, praying, listening to good uplifting, Godly music. Talking with disciplined followers of Christ. Working hard, doing the right thing.

Real Men Honor Women

A real man is someone who sees the world as it is, and as it should be. In popular culture, women are often portrayed as sex objects. Because of the blurred perceptions of a woman's sexuality, many women also allow and even participate in this stereotype. But God's plan is that men would honor women.

"Likewise, husbands, live together according to knowledge, giving honor to the wife as to the weaker vessel, the female, as truly being co-heirs together of the grace of life, not cutting off your prayers." (1 Peter 3:7 MKJV)

A great difference is made between men and women in this passage. Women are not weaker in the sense of equality with men. The difference here is the difference between clay pottery and fine china. Better said, men are like plastic ware and women are fine porcelain china. We are to treat them with respect and dignity and place them on a higher level of respect than we do other men.

My father taught me, when looking at a girl to remember, "She's someone's daughter, and someone's sister. One day she will be someone's mother. She should be treated with the same respect that you would show your mother, your daughter, or your sister."

The entire code of Chivalry dictates that a man use all his capabilities to protect and honor women.

For example:

A young man is meeting with a young lady and they are sitting across from each other. The young lady is wearing a low cut shirt that exposes her when she leans forward. The young man is faced with two choices. He can either wait for the opportune time to look at her with lust and try to see more, or he can tell her to please pull her shirt up. If he chooses to tell her, he communicates to her that he is a man of honor and he is protecting her honor.

God gave each man physical strength that is generally greater than a woman's strength. The purpose of that strength is never to overpower or harm, but always to be used to protect and uplift. God gave us greater physical strength and aggression so that we could physically protect women. As men, we are called to protect the honor of women as well.

"But I say to you that whoever looks on a woman to lust after her has already committed adultery with her in his heart." (Matthew 5:28 MKJV)

A great way to honor women is to refuse to see them as sex objects or something to abuse, but something to be honored and protected. To look at a woman with impure thoughts is not only a break of the Code of Chivalry, its breaking God's law. It's a big deal, even if popular culture says different. A great man honors women.

The King's Scroll

Romans 5:17 tells us that if we are men who have received the gift of God's grace, then we will reign like a King in life by Jesus Christ. The scripture says,

"For if, through the transgression of the one individual, Death made use of the one individual to seize the sovereignty, all the more shall those who receive God's overflowing grace and gift of righteousness reign as kings in Life through the one individual, Jesus Christ." Romans 5:17 (WNT)

Then in Deuteronomy, we are given a few guidelines of how a king is supposed to reign. We are told that one of the requirements of a king is that he is to write his own copy of the law. For me, that means that I am commanded to write key verses pertaining to those things that I face every day.

"And when he sits on the throne of his kingdom, he shall write for himself in a book a copy of this law, approved by the Levitical priests. 19 And it shall be with him, and he shall read in it all the days of his life, that he may learn to fear the LORD his God by keeping all the words of this law and these statutes, and doing them, 20 that his heart may not be lifted up above his brothers, and that he may not turn aside from the commandment, either to the right hand or to the left, so that he may continue long in his kingdom, he and his children, in Israel." (Deuteronomy 17:18 ESV)

A king will need extra help as he rules the Kingdom God gave him. To be a successful and good king, he will need guidance and encouragement from the word of God.

I know that as I go throughout the day, I struggle with feelings of lust, anger, depression, low self-esteem, feelings of inadequacy, hopelessness, and a lack of faith.

From these key verses, I learned to create a "Kings scroll" written out in my own handwriting that had key verses concerning each of these areas where I struggled. This scroll written by the King, was to be read by the king every day, to help him fear the Lord, stay on track, and avoid the pitfalls that trip up Kings.

The King's Seal

To remind me of my covenant as a King, I also placed crown symbols on my electronics; phone, ipad and computer. These visual reminders help me remember that as a king, I shouldn't look at inappropriate things on the Internet.

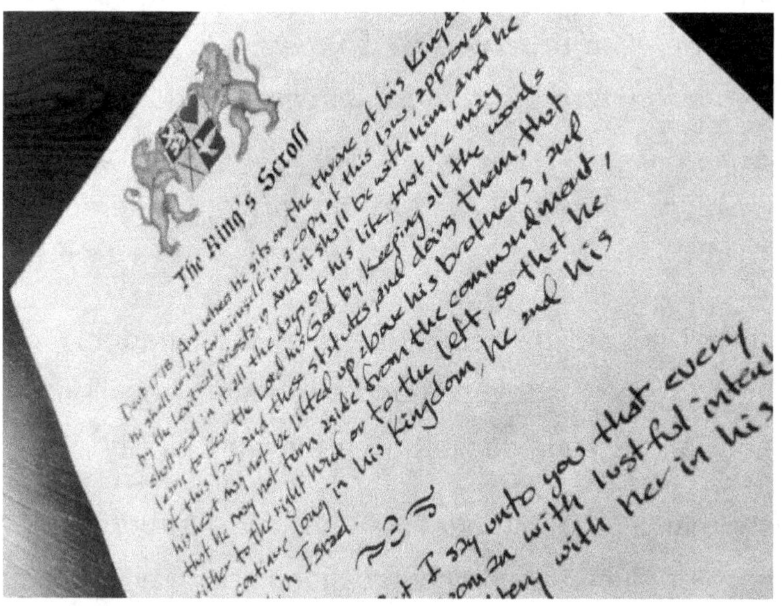

(My copy of The King's Scroll)

(The Crown sticker I placed on my Laptop)

Team Mission:

Identify key verses related to issues that you both struggle with. Be sure to include lust and sexual immorality.

____

____

____

____

____

____

Create a "Kings Scroll" for each of you using the key scriptures for items that challenge you.

Find crown stickers from Hobby Lobby or other craft or hobby shops. Place the stickers in key locations (on electronics, computers, monitors, etc.) to remind you of your covenant as a King.

LESSON 11

CHARACTER

It was an already hot and humid day in Belmopan, Belize at the Men of Honor camp we held there during the summer. We were gathered underneath a grass roofed, open air pavilion. The boys were singing worship songs at the end of our concluding service of the weekend camp. There had been amazing times at the camp and these young men's hearts had been deeply touched by God's presence.

One of the boys that attended the camp was from a really rough area near San Ignacio. He lived in a neighborhood that was populated with mostly shacks. One of the shacks that belonged to his friend sat on stilts and did not even have a front door, just an open doorway with a sheet hung in the opening. He was poor, even from a third-world perspective. He had come to the camp with no change of clothes, no bag, only an expectation of fun and great things happening. He was not disappointed. God showed up and filled his heart with His love and power. His face glowed with joy. After the service, he walked up to me and held out a clenched fist, palm downward as though he wanted to give me something. "What's this?" I asked. "The Lord told me to give this to you", he replied with a big smile on his brown face. He then turned his hand over and opened his hand toward me, revealing two crumpled one-dollar Belizean bills, and two coins. This was the equivalent of one U.S. Dollar. As I looked down at the money in his small hand my eyes then noticed, just below his outstretched hand, his toes sticking out from the end of two worn and filthy tennis shoes. In my mind I immediately thought, "How could I take this child's only money, when he so clearly needs it more than me?" Almost immediately in my heart I could hear the Lord saying, "You'd better take this precious offering! With this small amount, this young man is breaking the back of poverty and developing Christ-like character." I stopped, took the money, and prayed with the young man for him to receive a 100-fold return on his gift. A gift, though worth almost nothing to me and everything to him, would never be forgotten.

Character

"Your integrity is more important than your popularity." – Daniel Rorie

Four Key Points:

I.   Develop Your Character

II. Private Practice Determines Public Performance

III. Character is Displayed in the Small Things

IV. Act the Way you Want to Be

Four Key Verses:

I. *"Therefore the LORD God of Israel declares, 'I did indeed say that your house and the house of your father should walk before Me forever'; but now the LORD declares, 'Far be it from Me-- for those who honor Me I will honor, and those who despise Me will be lightly esteemed."* (1 Samuel 2:30 NASB)

II. *"Oh, the joys of those who do not follow the advice of the wicked, or stand around with sinners, or join in with mockers. But they delight in the law of the LORD, meditating on it day and night. Are like trees planted along the riverbank, bearing fruit each season. Their leaves never wither, and they prosper in all they do. But not the wicked! They are like worthless chaff, scattered by the wind. They will be condemned at the time of judgment. Sinners will have no place among the godly. For the LORD watches over the path of the godly, but the path of the wicked leads to destruction."* (Psalm 1)

III. *For our light, momentary affliction (this slight distress of the passing hour) is ever more and more abundantly preparing and producing and achieving for us an everlasting weight of glory [beyond all measure, excessively surpassing all comparisons and all calculations, a vast and transcendent glory and blessedness never to cease.], (2 Corinthians 4:17 AMP)*

IV. *"For God knew his people in advance, and he chose them to become like his Son, so that his Son would be the firstborn among many brothers and sisters."* (Romans 8: 29)

Develop Your Character

We have all been at one time or another, around or in contact with a person who displays strong character. And in every instance, we are taken back by the rarity of their character. Whether it is the person in the grocery store who gives back the extra change that they were given in error, or the person who does the right thing without accepting reward, we are moved by their example.

Our lives have been described in the Bible as being brief vapors. Life really flies by fast. We have been given a short span of years that are a testing ground to test the metal of our character. We have only one life to establish our character and create a reward that will follow us into the afterlife.

When we die, our character will be sealed, our history set, and eternity will be upon us. What will we have to show for our labors on the Earth? *Only our character.* What Legacy will we leave for our children and grandchildren?

Only our character. Will we have lived lives of Honor or a compromised existence of short cuts, half truths, and weak character?

Heavy or Light?

Hebrew scripture uses a great word to describe our lives of character. The word "Kebed" translates as "*to be heavy.*" I especially like the translation "*to have substance.*" Scripture almost always translates it as "*honor*" or "*glory.*" But when you think about character or honor what does it really mean but substance and weightiness.

"*Therefore the LORD God of Israel declares, 'I did indeed say that your house and the house of your father should walk before Me forever'; but now the LORD declares, 'Far be it from Me-- for those who honor Me I will honor, and those who despise Me will be lightly esteemed.* (1 Samuel 2:30 NASB)

The lives of every person can be summed up in this scripture. Either we honor the Lord or lightly esteem him, which means to think lightly. It is interesting that the word heavy and light is being used here.

Men who despise The Lord are careless about the afterlife and squander their time on Earth seeking foolish pleasures. Their souls will become empty or light, without substance.

Psalms Chapter 1 describes the wicked as "chaff that the wind blows away." In contrast, the righteous are described as trees that are planted, grounded, well watered, and solid.

"Oh, the joys of those who do not follow the advice of the wicked, or stand around with sinners, or join in with mockers. But they delight in the law of the LORD, meditating on it day and night. They are like trees planted along the riverbank, bearing fruit each season. Their leaves never wither, and they prosper in all they do. But not the wicked! They are like worthless chaff, scattered by the wind. They will be condemned at the time of judgment. Sinners will have no place among the godly. For the LORD watches over the path of the godly, but the path of the wicked leads to destruction." (Psalm 1)

Those who honor The Lord by displaying character will be honored. This literally means that He will attribute weightiness to them, more substance; a substance that will endure.

For our light, momentary affliction (this slight distress of the passing hour) is ever more and more abundantly preparing and producing and achieving for us an everlasting weight of glory [beyond all measure, excessively surpassing all comparisons and all calculations, a vast and transcendent glory and blessedness never to cease.], (2 Corinthians 4:17AMP)

Private Practice Determine Public Performance

We are the chief architects of our lives. We build our lives solid by building with character and integrity. We become men of substance by what we do when we think no one will know.

A very wealthy man hired a builder to build homes for him. The builder worked for many years for the man and built hundreds of homes. Over the years, the builder began to reason to himself that he had worked and made the man wealthier and began to resent the man for not paying him more.

One day, the wealthy man came to the builder and told him, "I want you to build me a really nice house. Money is no object; I will give you a half a million in cash to buy the materials. If you need more, just let me know." The builder began to reason that he deserved to make more and devised a plan to keep a portion of the money for himself.

When he started the foundation, he took short cuts on the steel rods and grade of concrete. When he did the framing, he used cheaper grades of board and less of them for support. He left insulation out of the walls in most areas, as no one would be able to see into the walls. He used low-grade electrical wire and hired unskilled labor to do the wiring. He cut every corner he could.

At the end of the build, he put heavier coats of paint over the work to hide the flaws. He ended up being able to steal several hundred dollars from the budget, and no one would know but him. The final day of the build came. The wealthy man showed up to the house and commended the builder for his fast and nice looking work. The builder handed the keys to the owner and told him that he spent the entire budget on the work.

The owner took the keys and smiling, handed them back to the builder. "I wanted to do something nice for you and your family for all your years of hard work - The house is for you." The builder had created a disaster for himself by building bad character into the house for himself and his family.

One of the marks of a great man is a man that can be depended upon to keep his word. Giving our word and keeping it means that we have integrity.

The word integrity has the same root as the word integrate. To have integrity means that I integrate the things that I think with the things I do. Those two things "integrate."

If I say its wrong to lie, yet I lie, I don't have integrity. If I say its wrong to steal, and yet I steal, I don't have integrity.

We demonstrate integrity by keeping our word and our actions in line with each other. God's word is true and you can count on Him to perform His word. As God's word is to Him, so our word should be to us.

Act the Way you Want to Be

There is an old saying, "Act the way you want to be, and soon you will be the way you act."

It's very true, whether we act in character or choose to do the wrong thing, we will become how we act.

I once heard the story about a young man who was born with a severely deformed face. The boy's mother, wanting to save him embarrassment and, I suppose, her as well, kept him out of the view of others. When he grew to the age of 5 and was old enough to go out and play with the other children, he experienced strange looks from the others, laughs and whispers about his strangely formed face. The boy quickly retreated into a life of seclusion in his house. One day, while playing in the attic, the boy came across a box containing several porcelain masks. He searched through the box until he found the mask of a handsome man. He tightly tied the mask on his own face, admiring himself in the mirror.

Day after day, the boy wore the mask and refused to take it off. It became his identity. After many years, the young man began to venture outside again. This time, he found and made friends. Although it seemed strange to them that the boy wore a mask, they found him interesting and friendly, so they accepted him.

Soon he met a young lady and they fell in love. She urged him to take off the mask. He refused.

One day a group of young men surrounded the couple. They insisted that he take off the mask. They threatened to take the mask off if he did not.

Slowly, reluctantly, he began to untie the mask.

The crowd waited in anticipation to see what lie behind this mask, hidden from them for so many years.

The young lady could scarcely bear to see what the true identity of the young man she had fallen in love with looked like.

As he slowly slid the mask from his face, the crowd was astonished to see, looking back at them, was the face of an even more handsome young man, whose face had been shaped to that of the mask, conformed into the image it had been pressed against for so many years.

God wants you to be conformed into the image of his son Jesus. The Bible tells us that He chose each one of us so that he could change us into His image.

"For God knew his people in advance, and he chose them to become like his Son, so that his Son would be the firstborn among many brothers and sisters." (Romans 8: 29)

The Lord wants to change or conform us into His image, and make us like Him.

Mission:

Dad:

Prepare to tell your son about a person from your family or from your past that has a character trait that you admire.

____

____

____

____

____

____

____

____

Son:

Share with your dad attributes and character traits of the man you hope to become. Ask your Dad to help you develop those areas and also hold you accountable to that plan.

____

____

____

____

____

____

Team Mission:

This exercise, while seeming morbid helps us to think about the things in life that matter most.

An obituary is a short description of a person's life that contains the best parts that describe a person. It is typically read at a person's funeral to celebrate the things about that person that highlight their character and life. Starting with the end in mind, each of you prepare a one-paragraph obituary that will sum up the things that you want to be remembered for most in your life.

My Obituary

____

____

____

____

____

____

____

____

____

____

LESSON 12

DECISION MAKING

Decision Making

One man that created his own world was the first person to reach billionaire status. This took place during the late 1800's. Every decision he made in life was strategic toward the goal of amassing incalculable wealth. Three years after reaching billionaire status, the 53 year old became gravely ill. He found himself in excruciating pain, unable to move and unable to enjoy the wealth he had gained. He lost all his hair. He was able to buy anything on the planet he wanted yet his only palatable meal became   crackers and milk. One of his friends noted, "He could not sleep, would not smile and nothing in life meant anything to him

The outlook for the man was very bleak and the world's best physicians predicted that he would not last through the year. The year grinded past painfully, slowly, and without improvement. As he neared the end of this year, he awoke suddenly with a vague remembrance of a dream he had during the night. Though he could not remember the details of the dream, the conclusion of the dream was that he would not be able to take his worldly success with him into the afterlife. He had to make a decision concerning his wealth and power. He called in attorneys, business managers, and accountants and instructed them that he wanted to direct his wealth toward making a difference with mission work, charitable contributions, medical research, and the betterment of his fellow man.

On that day in 1892, the idea for the Rockefeller Foundation began. Since the day it began to the present, the John D. Rockefeller Foundation has given over $14 billion in grants to organizations that would in turn lead to the discovery of penicillin, along with cures for diseases such as diphtheria, malaria, and tuberculosis.

Rockefeller's decision that day made great changes in the lives of others all over the world, but another interesting change took place. John D.'s body chemistry began to change from that very moment of decision and his health greatly improved. He soon completely recovered and lived to the ripe old age of 98!

Decision Making

"A father's responsibility is not to make his child's decisions, but to let the child watch him make his". –Ed Cole.

Four Key Points:

I. Decisions Should be Made Based on the Word of God.

II. Decisions Should be Made Based on Prayer.

III. Decisions Should be Made Based on Wise Counsel.

IV. Decisions Should be Made.

Four Key Verses

I. *"If you need wisdom, ask our generous God, and he will give it to you. He will not rebuke you for asking."* (James 1:5)

II. *"My sheep listen to my voice; I know them, and they follow me."* (John 10:27)

III. *"But the wisdom that is from above is first pure, then peaceable, gentle, and easy to be entreated, full of mercy and good fruits, without partiality, and without hypocrisy."* (James 3:17 KJV)

IV. *"Ask me and I will tell you remarkable secrets you do not know about things to come."* (Jeremiah 33:3)

One of the critical strengths of a man of substance is his ability to make decisions. Unfortunately, the decisions with the greatest impact often have to be made in the context of great pressure. Men who are great leaders throughout time have been men who made great decisions. The ability to make decisions is the mark of a real man. It's what we do. We make decisions. A man of strength is always counted on when times are tough to make decisions. Our wives and children look to us to make decisions. The decisions we make when we are children are easy and don't typically carry much consequences. But as we grow older, our decisions carry deeper consequences. For this reason, immature men avoid decision-making, or worse yet, make foolish decisions. That is why we must develop a foundation of knowledge to help us make decisions, and decision-making protocols that help us make sound decisions.

Former President Ronald Reagan tells the story about the time his Aunt took him to a shoemaker to have a pair of shoes made. The shoemaker asked young Reagan, "Do you want round toed shoes or squared?" Unable to decide, Reagan didn't answer, so the shoemaker gave him a few more days to decide. Several days later, the shoemaker saw Reagan on the street and asked him again whether he wanted round toes or squared. Reagan was still unable to decide, so the shoemaker told him, "Well, come by in a couple of days, and your shoes will be ready."

After a few days, Reagan went to the shoemakers shop only to find that he had made him one round and one squared toed shoe. "This will teach you to never let people make decisions for you." Reagan later said, "I learned right then and there, if you don't make your own decisions, someone else will!" (Today in the Word, MBI August 1991, pg.16)

Andrew Jackson was quoted as saying "Take time to deliberate; but when the time for action arrives, stop thinking, and go on."

If there is one thing that I have learned in my life that was important to pass to my son, it is that no decision should be based on emotion. All decisions should be made within a framework that eliminates bad choices and gives the most advantage to make a good decision.

Wise decisions can be made by using a few simple guidelines:

Decisions should be Made Based on The Word of God

God's word gives us very clear guidelines for every decision that we will make in life. If not exact in description, at least it is exact in intent of God's plan.

"Your word is a lamp to guide my feet and a light for my path." (Psalm 119:105)

One great way to gain practical wisdom in all matters that pertain to a man's life, whether personal, business, or relational, we can look to the book of Proverbs. We read the chapter of Proverbs that corresponds with the date. For example, if today's date is the 15th, we read Proverbs chapter 15. By doing this, because there are 31 chapters in Proverbs, we read through the entire book every month!

When you get financial advice, you wouldn't go to someone whose finances are a wreck, would you?

When you take your family to the doctor, you wouldn't go to someone who was not a degreed, certified, and experienced doctor, would you? Similarly, the book of Proverbs was written by a person who was called the wisest and wealthiest person to ever live. You are going to God's inspired word, written through a successful source. You can count on the advice being solid and trustworthy.

As you become a student of God's Word and read it daily, you will find practical advice on every subject. Also, many Bibles have a topical concordance that will help you find specific topics. If all else fails, consult your Pastor or church leader for specific locations for Bible promises and direction. God's way always works for the best.

Ed Cole once stated, "Our greatest freedom is the freedom to make decisions. But once we make the decision, we become a slave to that decision."

My Dad taught me that I am free to create my own world, but once I create it, I'll have to live in that world.

Decisions Should be Made based on Prayer

Who would want to march into a battle without the orders of their commanding officer?

Those officers, with the help of reconnaissance and technology know where the enemy is, and how best to engage him. With studies and proven battle strategy, they lay out the best course of action.

The same is true with our Heavenly Father. He knows the best course of action for our lives, has the best intentions in mind, and wants to show us how to win. The way that we get the strategy is in prayer.

Prayer is so often misunderstood as a one-way communication with God. God desires not only to hear our requests, but He wants to answer those requests and give His wise counsel. The only way we can get that advice is to listen. When we pray, we should expect to hear from God. It shows faith and just makes sense. Each critical decision that we make should be bathed in prayer.

Great men throughout time have used prayer in the course of their decision-making and seen God's hand move them to success. You are no different. If you pray and ask your father for direction, He will give it!

Judith Fain is a Ph.D. candidate at the University of Durham. As part of her studies, she spends several months each year in Israel. One day while walking on a road near Bethlehem, Judith watched as three shepherds converged with their separate flocks of sheep. The three men hailed each other and then stopped to talk. While they were conversing, their sheep intermingled, melting into one big flock.

Wondering how the three shepherds would ever be able to identify their own sheep, Judith waited until the men were ready to say their goodbyes. She watched, fascinated, as each of the shepherds called out to his sheep. At the sound of their shepherd's voice, like magic, the sheep separated again into three flocks. Apparently, some things in Israel haven't changed for thousands of years.

When we spend time in God's word and also in prayer, we become familiar with the voice and tone of God. This makes it easy when we hear the multitude of voices and thoughts speaking to us and leading us to choices. Because we have spent time with our Shepherd, we easily identify His voice and follow him.

My sheep listen to my voice; I know them, and they follow me. (John 10:27)

Decisions Should be Made Based on Wise Counsel

General George Armstrong Custer is a familiar name in military history. As commanding General of the famed 7th infantry, Custer was an up-and-coming military man. He reportedly decided to attack what he called a "small Indian village" on the banks of the Little Bighorn River.

In June of 1876, he was given (but ignored) the advice of General Alfred Terry to take another battalion and to make use of the new technology called the "Gatling Gun." This automatic weapon could fire 350 .45-.70 caliber rounds a minute. The force of 700 men approached the village of Chief Crazy Horse and a vastly underestimated force of Lakota braves.

A fierce battle ensued and the Indians annihilated Custer and his soldiers in what has since been named, "Custer's Last Stand." Military historians agree, had Custer taken the general's advice and taken the reinforcements and Gatling guns, he would have survived the battle of the Little Bighorn.

To ask for advice and admit need is never a sign of weakness, but rather a sign of wisdom.

"Plans go wrong for lack of advice; many advisers bring success." (Proverbs 15:22)

All decisions should be made with the benefit of wise counsel.

If there is time available to make an informed decision, it is always best to involve multiple advisors. A mentor or trusted advisor can offer valuable insights into decisions that we sometimes cannot see.

One of the 14 Leadership Traits of the Marine Corps is decisiveness. They state that decisiveness is defined as "able to make good decisions without delay. Get all the facts and weigh them against each other. By acting calmly and quickly, you should arrive at a sound decision. You announce your decisions in a clear, firm, professional manner."

Make a Decision

When faced with decisions, we must choose to make a decision based on what we know. To not make a decision is in itself a decision. Women like men who are decisive. Men follow other men who are decisive. When decisions present themselves, as men we should take the information we have and based on that information make a decision.

I like the old story of the indecisive judge:

In the courtroom, the prosecutor masterfully laid out the case against the defendant. He included all the accusations and evidence against the man. When he closed his arguments he said, "This man must be guilty!" To which the judge replied, "You're right!"

The defense attorney then masterfully presented the defense in great detail. At the end of his defense, he closed by saying, "So you see, your honor, the defendant MUST be innocent." To which the judge quickly replied, "You know what? You're right!"

The bailiff, having watched the case, the arguments, and the Judge's response to each, approached the bench. He whispered to the Judge, "Your honor, they can't BOTH be right." To which, the Judge replied, "You're right, you're right."

MISSION:

Dad:

Share a time when you had to make a hard decision. What was the outcome, what did you learn?

____

____

____

____

Son:

If there are decisions you need to make or foresee that you will have to make, ask your Dad to help you make those decisions using the strategy from this chapter.

____

____

____

____

____

Group Mission:

Write a list of possible key decisions that every man has to make in life. As a team, discuss how best to make these decisions and put a strategy in place to make them.

These decisions may include:

- Where am I going to college?
- How will I know whom to marry?
- What ministry will I do?
- What career will I choose?

____

____

____

____

____

____

____

____

____

____

____

LESSON 13

A FATHER'S

BLESSING

A Father's Blessing

It was a gloomy day in May 1940. Smoke from burning buildings filled the air. Their stomachs were empty and their clothes were ragged and worn out. The tired war-worn English troops had retreated as far as they could across France to finally arrive on the banks of the Thames River where they awaited evacuation.

The Nazis were roaring across France in full force with their Panzerschrek tanks, storm troopers, and dive-bombers. The Blitzkrieg or "lightning war" had begun and Hitler's full blood lust had been unleashed on Europe. These allied troops, with their back to the water waited anxiously for deliverance. But there was no deliverance in sight. They were completely pinned in and facing imminent danger. Through communication with the main allied force, they understood that there was capacity for only 25,000 troops to be evacuated by boat from the shores of France. That meant that 275,000, the bulk of the British forces, would face certain destruction at the hands of the Germans.

The English troops began to despair for their lives. Then a strange sight appeared on the horizon in the river Thames. It looked like little dots in the distance. Then as it grew closer, the soldiers could begin to make out the shapes of boats coming toward them. Over 800 ships sailed toward them in the distance. But these were no military vessels.

These were small boats, barges, yachts, canoes, fishing vessels and motorboats, dinghies and rowboats. The fathers of England had banded together in a most peculiar display armada of floating vessels. These fathers had come to rescue their sons. One by one the men swam out to chin depth water and climbed into the boats, all 300,000 piled onto these small boats as a miracle took place; a miracle that will go down as the largest civilian rescue operation in history, known as little ships of Dunkirk.

"As the Father has loved me, so have I love you." - Jesus

Four Key Points:

I. God Instituted the Father's Blessing

II. The Blessing is Passed from Father to Son

III. The Purpose of The Blessing

IV. The Blessing is A Rite of Passage

Four Key Verses:

I. *"This is my dearly loved Son who brings me great joy."* (Matthew 3:17).

II. *"These are the twelve tribes of Israel, and this is what their father said as he told his sons good-bye. He blessed each one with an appropriate message."* (Genesis 49:28)

III. *These commandments that I give you today are to be on your hearts. Impress them on your children. Talk about them when you sit at home and when you walk along the road, when you lie down and when you get up.* (Deuteronomy 6:6-7)

IV. *"He will restore the hearts of the fathers to their children and the hearts of the children to their fathers, so that I will not come and smite the land with a curse."* (Malachi 4:6 NASB)

It is important as we pass the torch to our sons, that we give them a clear and easily identifiable moment in time that we affirm them into manhood, with our blessing.

God Instituted the Father's Blessing

The blessing is a biblical pattern demonstrated throughout the scripture as it was passed from Father to Son. It began in the garden where God the Father formed Adam, not as when He had formed all of creation, but in a more relational, close, and intimate way. He formed man with His own hands out of the clay and dirt of the Earth and held man close to His face as He breathed the breath of life into Adam's nostrils. He then blessed Adam and told him to be fruitful.

The Blessing is Passed form Father to Son

God also blessed Abraham and pronounced a blessing upon him. Abraham blessed Isaac and Isaac in turn blessed Jacob. So the blessing has been passed from Father to Son since the creation of the world. It is God's perfect plan that this blessing is passed from father to son continually.

One great example of how a Father's Blessing should look is found in the movie "Flywheel." In this scene, the father comes to the son's office and prays for and pronounces blessing over his son. This excerpt from the movie is used to illustrate a Father's Blessing in our Men of Honor camps all around the world. You can view it via YouTube here: http://youtube.com/BCAyBLP4kSo

The Purpose of The Blessing

The blessing has one over-arching effect; it reverses the curse. Where there is no blessing, the curse remains. We see it demonstrated by God sending His spirit to turn the hearts of the fathers to their children, and the hearts of the children to their fathers, unless He smite the Earth with a curse in Malachi 4:6. Where there is no blessing, there is a curse.

Fathers either bless their sons or the sons walk in the curse of fatherlessness.

The effects of the father's blessing are evident and bring great benefits to the son in every instance. With Abraham, he became so rich that there wasn't enough room in the land for him to share space with another. The same thing happened when he passed it down to his son. Even his grandson, once blessed, planted crops during a time of severe drought and famine and reaped one hundred fold.

The blessing is not based on performance or merit, but merely on sonship. God himself demonstrated the blessing of His Son at Jordan where Jesus, who had not yet performed a miracle, received his Father's blessing. God the Father blessed His Son by saying, "This is my dearly loved Son who brings me great joy." (Matthew 3:17).

It was this blessing that solidified identity and carried Jesus through his time of temptation in the wilderness. The enemy tried to get Jesus to question His own identity by saying, "If you really are the Son of God..."

Jesus had a clear and easily identifiable moment that he could remember, *"I am my Father's Son and I bring Him great joy!"*

The Blessing is A Rite of Passage

Great cultures around the world call their young men out of childhood into manhood in some very creative ways. These activities called "rites of passage" give a young man a clear and definitive "line in the sand" to reference and help them to remember the day they entered manhood. These rites can be extreme like the Vanuatu warriors who "bungee" jump headlong from a wooden platform to the ground hundreds of feet below with only hand picked vines wrapped around their ankles, or the West African scarification rituals where the forehead is cut repeatedly with long lines to indicate a transition into manhood. They can also be like the Cherokee warrior entrance into manhood:

"His father takes him into the forest, blindfolds him, and leaves him alone. He is required to sit on a stump the whole night and not remove the blindfold until the rays of the morning sun shine through it. He cannot cry out for help to anyone. Once he survives the night, he is a MAN. He cannot tell the other boys of this experience, because each lad must come into manhood on his own. The boy is naturally terrified. He can hear all kinds of noises. Wild beasts must surely be all around him. Maybe even some human might do him harm. The wind blew the grass and earth, and shook his stump, but he sat stoically, never removing the blindfold. It would be the only way he could become a man. Finally, after a horrific night, the sun appeared and he removed his blindfold. It was then that he discovered his father sitting on the stump next to him. He had been at watch the entire night, protecting his son from harm."

The culture in which I was raised had some very unhealthy and unclear rites of passage. They were neither significant nor appropriate for my entrance into manhood. As a result, I struggled and often questioned, "Do I have what it takes to be a man?" They were things like the first time I had drank a beer, or the first time I had sex. These types of rites of passage don't require manhood, just being a male. Afterward, they also only leave you feeling less like a man compared to how you felt before you did them.

How I Passed the Torch

It was 6 months before Daniel turned 13. I realized that in Jewish society a young man was regarded as a man when he reached 13. I wanted to give my son a rite of passage that would be a night to remember for all his life, and pass on to his son when he became a father. I wanted to give Daniel a powerful and meaningful entrance into manhood. I reached out to every man that I knew and respected to be a Godly and significant man in Daniel's life.

I chose twenty men to be a part of Daniel's entrance into manhood ceremony. The twenty included his Grandfather, Pastors, Youth Pastors, his Men of Honor group leaders, uncles, and friends of our family who were men of character and strength.

For the location, I chose the ranch of a friend, out in the middle of *A Few Miles from Nowhere,* Texas. (*Actually it was an hour East of Dallas, TX*) The ranch had a great rock patio where we could gather around a bonfire, cook steaks, and celebrate Daniel's special night.

I prepared these men in advance by asking them to come prepared with a quick (one-minute) description of one attribute that they could see and affirm already in Daniel's character and also one area that they would encourage him in as he prepared to become a man.

The night finally came. We gathered at the Ranch at about 6PM as the sun was setting. We grilled steaks and baked potatoes in this rustic ranch setting during the cool Texas early spring. It was a beautiful night.

After we ate, we gathered solemnly around the bonfire where we could hear clearly and each man could look Daniel directly in the eye and share their heart with him. Each man shared the strengths they saw in Daniel with him. They spoke of purity, strength, Godliness, and joy. After each man had shared their word of affirmation, they began to share their words of encouragement about aspects of manhood. These aspects were humility, honor, faithfulness, friendship, and intimacy with God. Daniel was being filled with the best, *by the best.*

Finally, it came time for his grandfather to share his perspective with Daniel. My dad chose to share with Daniel the aspect of Courage. When my dad got halfway into his talk on courage, something memorable and amazing happened. It is something that none of us will ever forget.

What we didn't know is that my friend Cam's Ranch was situated next to another ranch that specialized in the rescue of large cats. When I say large cats, I mean really large cats, like tigers and Lions.

When my Dad mentioned the word Courage, as if on cue, one of the Lions loudly roared. Everyone's eyes widened. People began to mouth to each other, "Was that a Lion?" I could not have paid to have such a powerful emphasis of the word courage as to have that Lion roar almost in response to the word courage. It was as if God himself had spoken a word of affirmation.

After my Dad finished his word for Dan, it was my turn to finish the night. I had Daniel take a knee in the center of this circle of men. I brought out two gifts to commemorate this special night. The first gift was a sword that I had purchased for him. It was really big and really sharp. I laid the sword across his opened hands. Then I handed him a second sword. This was the sword of the Lord, a Bible with his name written in gold on the front and the phrase "a MAN after God's own heart" written beneath his name. I then prayed for Dan that God would help him to become a powerful man. I prayed that Daniel's heart would always be fierce, bold, and seeking after God. Then, I called him into manhood. I told him that he had kneeled as a boy, but now he would stand as a man. When Daniel stood the men shouted and clapped for him. Daniel had become a man. He would never forget, and neither would we, that special night he was called into manhood.

A fathers blessing and affirmation is critical to the formation of a son into a man. We create a godly legacy that can be passed for generations when we create these events for our sons. It's never too late to have a ceremony for your son. Whether he's 13 or 25, you can do the same. Make it special. But even if its just you praying with him, he'll never forget or lack for his father's blessing.

Conclusion:

As fathers, we want to make sure our sons become strong men. When my son was born, I began to take a mental inventory of all that I would need to train and help him learn the necessary lessons of manhood. I really wondered if I had all the correct insight to help him avoid all the traps that lie ahead of him, and especially *the traps that caught me.* I also wondered if I would be able to give him the right tools to navigate manhood and become a much better and more successful man than I became. Did I have the right stuff to put in him? I think all good Dads feel the same way. That's probably why you read this book.

For the short season that we have our sons in our care, we are working with wet concrete. To help our sons become strong and successful, we have a very narrow window in which to work. The good news is, whether he's 9 or 19, *it's not too late to start.*

This 13-week experience is a biblical study of key elements of manhood and masculinity. It is designed to help you begin conversations with your son – whether he's with you all the time, or you only see him on the weekends – in order to help him form a strong foundation for manhood.

Another intended use is to help you mentor a spiritual son. With the lack of fathers today, it becomes a great opportunity for us to help those who don't have dads. We can become surrogate fathers for those young men who don't have a strong father figure in their lives.

A great example in the Bible is Paul and Timothy. Paul called Timothy, "my dear son" though he was not his biological father. Whether you are going through this 13-week study with your biological son or grandson, step son, or spiritual son, I pray that this book and the subsequent journey for you and your son becomes a bright torch that will be handed down in families for generations to come. When thinking about passing the torch, I really like the quote by George Bernard Shaw:

> *"This is the true joy in life, the being used for a purpose recognized by yourself as a mighty one; the being a force of nature instead of a feverish, selfish little clod of ailments and grievances complaining that the world will not devote itself to making you happy.*
> *I am of the opinion that my life belongs to the whole community, and as long as I live it is my privilege to do for it whatever I can.*

I want to be thoroughly used up when I die, for the harder I work the more I live. I rejoice in life for its own sake. Life is no "brief candle" for me. It is a sort of splendid torch which I have got hold of for the moment, and I want to make it burn as brightly as possible before handing it on to future generations."

-George Bernard Shaw

The race of manhood is not a singular sprint, but a relay race. In order to win the race, we must successfully pass the torch to the next generation.

This study may also aptly be named "Passing the Flame", because the full intent for us as fathers is to pass the torch of manhood to the next generation in an intentional way, while understanding that we must continue strong to the end carrying the torch of manhood.

Authentic and biblical masculinity is an increasingly rare thing in our world today. Some "men" want to be women and some "women" desire to be men. Often because someone has failed to effectively pass the torch of manhood to the next generation.

Authentic manhood is lacking in men today and the effects on our society are devastating.

It is time for men to be what they were created to be; strong, manly, and good. And it's also time for us men to pass that on to the next generation in a meaningful and intentional way.

Manhood is sometimes a bit dangerous. Manhood is never reckless, but sometimes dangerous. And that is something that only a man can communicate to his son. While it is true that mothers can pass on spirituality to boys, only a father can impart masculinity.

There are many definitions of manhood presented as authentic manhood, but there can only be one.

Every culture throughout time has defined manhood for that culture. Some were based on feats of strength, some on age. Some definitions were based on sexual prowess, and some on completion of a rite-of-passage. These definitions of manhood, although comprised of some element of masculine strength or ability, fail to correctly define manhood. There can only be one standard for defining manhood.

I sought for many years to find exactly what it meant to be a man. I was told that when I could fight and win, I would be a man; I was told that if I could drink and hold my liquor, I would be a man; I was even told that when I was able to have sex with a girl, I would be a man.

I found out that according to the popular definition of manhood, I could fulfill that definition and could also be a drunken idiot, in jail, with a venereal disease or have an unplanned pregnancy. Sadly, I was still not a man. Their definitions were lacking in every area, especially in the area of truth.

That is why it is of utmost importance that we as men understand the truth and convey that truth to the next generation.

My father, for the most part, taught me most of the lessons concerning manhood and through words and example taught me how a man should live, and also die. He was a transformed example for everyone to see. Prior to his salvation, he roofed houses during the day and closed the bars down at 2 a.m. most nights. He was a rough, tough, bar brawler who enjoyed a fight. My father gave his heart fully to Christ when I was 19 and for the next 26 years, he lived his life pursuing God. His favorite verse was Galatians 2:20 that says,

My old self has been crucified with Christ. It is no longer I who live, but Christ lives in me. So I live in this earthly body by trusting in the Son of God, who loved me and gave himself for me."

My dad lived that verse to the full, right up to his last moment.

His favorite verse was Galatians 2:20 and at 2:20 in the afternoon on Feb. 20 (2/20) he took his last breath here on Earth and the next breath in the presence of the King of Kings. That's how a real man puts an exclamation mark on his life! He taught me how to live, and finally, how to die.

This book is not intended to be an exhaustive source on all aspects of manhood, but rather a facilitation of meaningful conversations between fathers and sons that convey truth.

Most fathers deeply desire to pass the very best to their children and this study is meant to ensure that fathers and sons have the opportunity to discuss the things that matter most. My great hope is that you will develop a stronger and richer relationship with your son, and you will have a confidence in knowing that he's ready for the things he will soon face in his journey into manhood.

A man whose heart is fully alive and full of the essence of Biblical masculinity is a majestic and rare sight to see. My hope is that you revel in your manhood and pass it on to your son in a clear and meaningful way, so that it takes root and even increases in him.

Strength & Honor!

Tony Rorie

August 2014

About The Author:

Tony Rorie is the founder of the Men & Ladies of Honor Youth Character Education Program, a program that began in 2003 while he was working as an administrator and then Principal of a public school district with over 1,500 students in the Pleasant Grove area of Dallas, TX. The program has impacted thousands of students.

While the program began with mentoring just four boys after school in Dallas, TX, it has grown to locations in Michigan, Florida, Mississippi, California, and 5 other countries including Belize and South Africa.

Tony is a veteran youth pastor and communicator with a passion for turning the hearts of the Fathers to the children and the hearts of the children to the Fathers.

He is an author and motivational speaker whose works include *"**Raise Sons**: God's Strategy for Reaching Generation Next"* and *"**The Quest**: Becoming a Man of Honor"*.

He and Melissa have been special guests on national television programs and received critical acclaim for their work with men and youth.

Tony and Melissa live in Dallas, TX and were married in 1990. They have three children who are involved in the work of the ministry alongside them.

Tony conducts camps, travels, and speaks in churches and at men's retreats challenging men to father the next generation.

For additional information, write:

Tony Rorie

PO Box 1341

Rowlett, TX 75030

tonyrorie@themenofhonor.org

www.tonyrorie.com

Attribution:

Chapter 1: Picture of Young Theodore Roosevelt
http://www.britannica.com/EBchecked/topic/509347/Theod
ore-Roosevelt

Chapter 2: Courage MLK Photo:
http://www.easternstate.org/explore/tour-guide-
chronicles/seeing-mlk-first-time

Page 22: Aslan passage from "The Lion,
The Witch, and the Wardrobe by C.S. Lewis

 Pg 44: New Man, March/April 1997, p. 18

Chapter 3 Story Told by Ronald Reagan
(http://www.presidency.ucsb.edu/ws/?pid=39099)

Good Timber - Douglas Malloch, Quoted in Resource,
Sept./Oct., 1992, p. 7

Reference for Cherokee Rite of Passage:
https://nuwatiherbals.com/traditions/

from Lois Tverberg's blog, (pg 154)
http://ourrabbijesus.com/articles/discipleship-not-fences-
but-following-shepherd/

http://marines.dodlive.mil/2011/03/22/the-marine-corps-
14-leadership-traits-decisiveness/ (page 157)

Chapter 4 Opening Story by Michael Rogers:
http://www.teamworkandleadership.com/category/leadership-stories-series#sthash.kPapTczx.dpbs

Chapter 5 Picture of Tomb of the Unknown:
http://images.christianpost.com/full/56318/honor-guards-stand-on-duty-at-the-tomb-of-the-unknown-soldier-in-sept-2012-in-arlington-county-va.jpg

Chapter 6 Picture of Lt. Michael Murphy:http://www.veteransunited.com/network/michael-murphy-seal-makes-distress-call-in-storm-of-enemy-fire/

Pg 73: Source www.navy.mil/moh/mpmurphy

Chapter 7 Picture of Ford, Edison
http://iconicphotos.files.wordpress.com/2009/05/ford_edison_harding_and_firestone_new_york_times_1921.jpg

Chapter 8:
Picture of Samurai:
Hand-coloured print from the 1870s (Photo: Peabody Museum, Harvard)

Benjamin Franklin list of virtues from:
http://thirteenvirtues.com

Chapter 12: Decision making. Story of founding of Rockefeller Foundation from
http://www.kluth.org/church/illustrations.htm

And http://www.rockefellerfoundation.org/about-us/our-history

Chapter 13: Father's Blessing Clip from:

https://www.youtube.com/watch?v=BCAyBLP4kSo